1980s Project Studies/Council on Foreign Relations

DIVERSITY AND DEVELOPMENT IN SOUTHEAST ASIA:

The Coming Decade

Studies by Guy J. Pauker, Frank H. Golay, and Cynthia H. Enloe

NUCLEAR WEAPONS AND WORLD POLITICS:

Alternatives for the Future

Studies by David C. Gompert, Michael Mandelbaum, Richard L. Garwin, and John H. Barton

CHINA'S FUTURE:

Foreign Policy and Economic Development in the Post-Mao Era

Studies by Allen S. Whiting and Robert F. Dernberger

ALTERNATIVES TO MONETARY DISORDER

Studies by Fred Hirsch and Michael W. Doyle and by Edward L. Morse

NUCLEAR PROLIFERATION:

Motivations, Capabilities, and Strategies for Control

Studies by Ted Greenwood and by Harold A. Feiveson and Theodore B. Taylor

INTERNATIONAL DISASTER RELIEF:

Toward a Responsive System

Stephen Green

STUDIES FORTHCOMING

The 1980s Project will comprise about 25 volumes. Most will contain independent but related studies concerning issues of potentially great importance in the next decade and beyond, such as resource management, human rights, population studies, and relations between the developing and developed societies, among many others. Additionally, a number of volumes will be devoted to particular regions of the world, concentrating especially on political and economic development trends outside the industrialized West.

Sharing Global Resources

Sharing Global Resources

Ruth W. Arad and Uzi B. Arad

Rachel McCulloch and José Piñera

Ann L. Hollick

Introduction by Edward L. Morse

1980s Project/Council on Foreign Relations

McGRAW-HILL BOOK COMPANY

New York   St. Louis   San Francisco
Auckland Bogotá Düsseldorf Johannesburg London Madrid
Mexico Montreal New Delhi Panama Paris São Paulo
Singapore Sydney Tokyo Toronto

The Council on Foreign Relations, Inc., is a nonprofit and nonpartisan organization devoted to promoting improved understanding of international affairs through the free exchange of ideas. Its membership of about 1,700 persons throughout the United States is made up of individuals with special interest and experience in international affairs. The Council has no affiliation with and receives no funding from the United States government.

The Council publishes the journal *Foreign Affairs* and, from time to time, books and monographs that in the judgment of the Council's Committee on Studies are responsible treatments of significant international topics worthy of presentation to the public. The 1980s Project is a research effort of the Council; as such, 1980s Project Studies have been similarly reviewed through procedures of the Committee on Studies. As in the case of all Council publications, statements of fact and expressions of opinion contained in 1980s Project Studies are the sole responsibility of their authors.

The editor of this book was Tita Gillespie for the Council on Foreign Relations. Thomas Quinn and Michael Hennelly were the editors for McGraw-Hill Book Company. Christopher Simon was the designer, and Teresa Leaden supervised the production. This book was set in Times Roman by Offset Composition Services, Inc.

Printed and bound by R. R. Donnelley and Sons.

Library of Congress Cataloging in Publication Data

Main entry under title:

Sharing global resources.

(1980s Project/Council on Foreign Relations)
Bibliography: p.
Includes index.
1. Natural resources—Addresses, essays, lectures.
2. Commercial policy—Addresses, essays, lectures.
3. Maritime law—Addresses, essays, lectures.
4. World politics—1975–1985—Addresses, essays, lectures.   I.   Arad, Ruth W.   II.   Series: Council on Foreign Relations.   1980s Project/Council on Foreign Relations.

HC55.S44   333.7   78-13233
ISBN 0-07-002150-3
ISBN 0-07-002151-1 pbk.
1 2 3 4 5 6 7 8 9 R R D R R D 7 9 8 7 6 2 1 0 9

Contents

List of Tables

Foreword: The 1980s Project

The dependence of many developing countries upon export earnings from commodities and raw materials whose prices vary greatly from year to year, the example of "commodity power" set by OPEC in the mid-1970s, a growing concern over raw material shortages, and new issues of equity in a range of international negotiations have increased the prominence of the role played by resources in international affairs. The three essays in this volume examine the need for developing new patterns for the international management of resources. They are part of a stream of studies commissioned by the 1980s Project of the Council on Foreign Relations, each of which analyzes issues that are likely to be of international concern during the next 10 to 20 years.

The ambitious purpose of the 1980s Project is to examine important political and economic problems not only individually but in relationship to one another. Some studies or books produced by the Project will primarily emphasize the interrelationship of issues. In the case of other, more specifically focused studies, a considerable effort has been made to write, review, and criticize them in the context of more general Project work. Each Project study is thus capable of standing on its own; at the same time it has been shaped by a broader perspective.

The 1980s Project had its origin in the widely held recognition that many of the assumptions, policies, and institutions that have characterized international relations during the past 30 years are inadequate to the demands of today and the foreseeable demands of the period between now and 1990 or so. Over the course of the next decade, substantial adaptation of institutions and behavior will be needed to respond to the changed circumstances of the 1980s and beyond. The Project seeks to identify those future conditions and the kinds of adaptation they might require. It is not the Project's purpose to arrive at a single or exclusive set of goals. Nor does it focus upon the foreign policy or national interests of the United States alone. Instead, it seeks to identify goals that are compatible with the perceived interests of most states, despite differences in ideology and in level of economic development.

The published products of the Project are aimed at a broad readership, including policy makers and potential policy makers and those who would influence the policy-making process, but are confined to no single nation or region. The authors of Project studies were therefore asked to remain mindful of interests broader than those of any one society and to take fully into account the likely realities of domestic politics in the principal societies involved. All those who have worked on the Project, however, have tried not to be captives of the status quo; they have sought to question the inevitability of existing patterns of thought and behavior that restrain desirable change and to look for ways in which those patterns might in time be altered or their consequences mitigated.

The 1980s Project is at once a series of separate attacks upon a number of urgent and potentially urgent international problems and also a collective effort, involving a substantial number of persons in the United States and abroad, to bring those separate approaches to bear upon one another and to suggest the kinds of choices that might be made among them. The Project involves more than 300 participants. A small central staff and a steering Coordinating Group have worked to define the questions and to assess the compatibility of policy prescriptions. Nearly 100 authors, from more than a dozen countries, have been at work on separate studies. Ten working groups of specialists and generalists have been convened to subject the Project's studies to critical scrutiny and to help in the process of identifying interrelationships among them.

The 1980s Project is the largest single research and studies effort the Council on Foreign Relations has undertaken in its 55-year history, comparable in conception only to a major study of the postwar world, the War and Peace Studies, undertaken by the Council during the Second World War. At that time, the impetus of the effort was the discontinuity caused by worldwide conflict and the visible and inescapable need to rethink, replace, and supplement many of the features of the international system that had prevailed before the war. The discontinuities in today's world are less obvious and, even when occasionally quite visible—as in the abandonment of gold convertibility and fixed monetary parities—only briefly command the spotlight of public attention. That new institutions and patterns of behavior are needed in many areas is widely acknowledged, but the sense of need is less urgent—existing institutions have not for the most part dramatically failed and collapsed. The tendency, therefore, is to make do with outmoded arrangements and to improvise rather than to undertake a basic analysis of the problems that lie before us and of the demands that those problems will place upon all nations.

The 1980s Project is based upon the belief that serious effort and integrated forethought can contribute—indeed, are indispensable—to progress in the next decade toward a more humane, peaceful, productive, and just world. And it rests upon the hope that participants in its deliberations and readers of Project publications—whether or not they agree with an author's point of view—may be helped to think more informedly about the opportunities and the dangers that lie ahead and the consequences of various possible courses of future action.

The 1980s Project has been made possible by generous grants from the Ford Foundation, the Lilly Endowment, the Andrew W. Mellon Foundation, the Rockefeller Foundation, and the German Marshall Fund of the United States. Neither the Council on Foreign Relations nor any of those foundations is responsible for statements of fact and expressions of opinion contained in publications of the 1980s Project; they are the sole responsibility of the individual authors under whose names they appear. But the Council on Foreign Relations and the staff of the 1980s Project take great pleasure in placing those publications before a wide readership both in the United States and abroad.

The 1980s Project

1980s PROJECT WORKING GROUPS

During 1975 and 1976, ten Working Groups met to explore major international issues and to subject initial drafts of 1980s Project studies to critical review. Those who chaired Project Working Groups were:

Cyrus R. Vance, Working Group on Nuclear Weapons and Other Weapons of Mass Destruction

Leslie H. Gelb, Working Group on Armed Conflict

Roger Fisher, Working Group on Transnational Violence and Subversion

Rev. Theodore M. Hesburgh, Working Group on Human Rights

Joseph S. Nye, Jr., Working Group on the Political Economy of North-South Relations

Harold Van B. Cleveland, Working Group on Macroeconomic Policies and International Monetary Relations

Lawrence C. McQuade, Working Group on Principles of International Trade

William Diebold, Jr., Working Group on Multinational Enterprises

Eugene B. Skolnikoff, Working Group on the Environment, the Global Commons, and Economic Growth

Miriam Camps, Working Group on Industrial Policy

1980s PROJECT STAFF

Persons who have held senior professional positions on the staff of the 1980s Project for all or part of its duration are:

Miriam Camps	*Catherine Gwin*
William Diebold, Jr.	*Roger D. Hansen*
Tom J. Farer	*Edward L. Morse*
David C. Gompert	*Richard H. Ullman*

Richard H. Ullman was Director of the 1980s Project from its inception in 1974 until July 1977, when he became Chairman of the Project Coordinating Group, Edward L. Morse was Executive Director from July 1977 until June 1978. At that time, Catherine Gwin, 1980s Project Fellow since 1976, took over as Executive Director.

PROJECT COORDINATING GROUP

The Coordinating Group of the 1980s Project had a central advisory role in the work of the Project. Its members as of June 30, 1978, were:

Carlos F. Díaz-Alejandro
Richard A. Falk
Tom J. Farer
Edward K. Hamilton
Stanley Hoffmann
Gordon J. MacDonald
Bruce K. MacLaury

Bayless Manning
Theodore R. Marmor
Ali Mazrui
Michael O'Neill
Stephen Stamas
Fritz Stern
Allen S. Whiting

Until they entered government service, other members included:

W. Michael Blumenthal
Richard N. Cooper
Samuel P. Huntington

Joseph S. Nye, Jr.
Marshall D. Shulman

COMMITTEE ON STUDIES

The Committee on Studies of the Board of Directors of the Council on Foreign Relations is the governing body of the 1980s Project. The Committee's members as of June 30, 1978, were:

Barry E. Carter
Robert A. Charpie
Stanley Hoffmann
Henry A. Kissinger
Walter J. Levy

Robert E. Osgood
Stephen Stamas
Paul A. Volcker
Marina v. N. Whitman

James A. Perkins (Chairman)

Sharing Global Resources

Introduction: The International Management of Resources

Edward L. Morse

Almost every list of "new" international issues drawn up in recent years would have included "oil power" or "commodity power" or "the politics of scarcity" and the "North-South" dialogue. Although scares about resource depletion have cropped up from time to time during this century, none seemed so critically important to governments or citizens as that which occurred in the 1970s. Three particular themes associated with resources drew a great deal of public and political attention to their role in international affairs:

- Accompanying the worldwide economic boom of the early 1970s was an extraordinary growth in demand for resources, especially in the Western industrial countries, which resulted not only in supply shortages but also in dramatic and inflationary "explosions" in the prices of grains, minerals, and other raw materials. By happenstance, these shortfalls in supply occurred at the same time that the Club of Rome and other visible groups of publicists generated widespread belief that the world economy was quickly reaching the physical limits to growth, painting a bleak Malthusian scenario about a long-term problem of supply across a broad range of commodities which would bring to an end an age of abundance.

- The ability of OPEC to quadruple the nominal price of oil in 1973, and of some Arab members of OPEC to exercise the "oil weapon" by withholding petroleum through selective boycotts of the United States and some other oil importers, inspired other governments in the developing world to investigate the potential of their own commodity power. Although developed countries such as the United States, Australia, and Canada are the major producers and exporters of a wide range of commodities, for the developing countries a much larger—indeed a predominant—share of exports is in natural resources and other commodities. The developing countries therefore had a special incentive to try to wield commodity power for essentially instrumental purposes: to induce a greater transfer of resources from the Western industrial countries, to increase the voice of developing countries in the management of international trade and thereby to bias the international trading system more in favor of the needs of the developing world, and, at least for some developing countries, to achieve enhanced power, status, and prestige in the international arena.

- Although complaints about adverse terms of trade affecting their exports of commodities and raw materials had been voiced by developing countries for more than a decade, the quest for greater equity in the international economy placed the management of resources at the center of discussions and negotiations of a new international economic order. Funds for buffer stocks, schemes for compensatory finance for shortfalls in export earnings, and other methods to stabilize income for developing countries were seriously proposed and debated by governments of developing and industrial societies as an integral part of the North-South dialogue.

Clearly, acute but short-lived shortages of a wide variety of commodities in the early 1970s fed into the academic fashion associated with the revival of Malthusianism and lent credibility to the notion that developing countries could exercise commodity power to achieve a more equitable international economic order. When attention is turned to the coming decade and beyond, few predictions about resource-related issues can be made with any certainty. The shortages of a few years ago rapidly disappeared as the industrial societies of the West entered into a persistent recession, as businesses accumulated large inventories of commodities, and as new sources of supply came into being. OPEC's experience in wielding commodity power now appears to be not only unique but perhaps more constrained by market forces than many persons expected, as efforts at conservation begin to be taken more seriously in importing countries, as new sources of energy are discovered, and as the OPEC countries themselves lose their freedom of action as a result of their increased involvement in the world economy. And after a brief flurry of negotiating activity, international arrangements to manage resource flows as part of a more equitable international economic order have been less easy to create than many of their earlier proponents had originally thought, in part because what can be agreed upon leaves aside the most difficult issues.

The essays in this volume address themselves to these and other uncertainties about the role resources are likely to play in international affairs during the coming decade and beyond. As well, their authors put forward proposals designed not only to defuse international conflicts over the control of resources but also to achieve more equitable international arrangements for dealing with the effects on costs and income of excesses and shortfalls of traded commodities associated with large swings in supply and demand.

In the first essay, Ruth W. Arad and Uzi B. Arad, both of Tel Aviv University, analyze the bases of commodity power and assess the likelihood that international conflicts will arise over access to resources. On the whole their conclusions are bleak for those proponents of a new international economic order who see in the manipulation of the supply of resources a way to assure a transformation in the hierarchy of status and power in international society. Their analysis, however, leads to relatively reassuring conclusions for those who fear the outbreak of conflicts over access to resources.

Rachel McCulloch of Harvard University and José Piñera of the Catholic University of Santiago, Chile, examine in the second essay alternative means by which trade in commodities might be managed, bearing in mind both the benefits and the imperfections of competitive markets in this area. They examine the degree to which current trading arrangements satisfy four basic objectives: fair distribution of benefits, efficiency, stability, and security of both markets and sources of supply, and they conclude that people in both industrial and developing countries would benefit substantially from a revision and strengthening of trading rules. They also examine the case put forward by developing countries for manipulating commodity markets in order to enhance a transfer of wealth from rich to poor societies. They reject a pure laissez faire policy, which, given imbalances in both production and consumption, they believe to be unsatisfactory. Instead they urge, at a minimum, the adoption of a number of proposals that would be adapted to the market structure of individual commodities. These include an internationally managed insurance scheme to stabilize export earnings; improvement, through subsidization, of futures markets to smooth out fluctuations in price; the elimination of trade restrictions, especially those imposed by industrial countries; and the expansion of processing activities in developing countries, in part through the elimination of cascaded tariffs in importing societies.

Furthermore, McCulloch and Piñera suggest more far-reaching and fundamental changes in their "ideal regime" for commodity trade. Although these proposals for structural change appear to entail higher costs to both Northern and Southern countries, they argue that, in the long run, both market efficiency and the prospects for more rapid economic growth would benefit all societies. These more extensive proposals include the levying of an international tax on commodity trade as a means of redistributing income to poorer exporters and the negotiation of new rules to increase market competitiveness and to reduce collusion among—and between—consumers and producers. The costs of these proposals should not be minimized, since they would entail substantial sacrifice of national sovereignty. Moreover, as McCulloch and Piñera point out, unless great care is taken in working out the details of the tax scheme, the distributional costs could well be borne by those countries they were designed to benefit. Whether or not the ideal model proposed by the authors is feasible, it provides a set of goals—quite distinct from current negotiations on a Common Fund for financing buffer-stock agreements—that could help to structure negotiations over more modest changes.

The third essay in this volume, by Ann L. Hollick of the Johns Hopkins School of Advanced International Studies, examines an area of rapid international change that is currently the subject of intense negotiations: the emerging law concerning the regulation of access to—and use of—ocean space. Although issues concerned with the law of the seas touch upon national security concerns and reflect many peripheral aspects of the North-South dialogue, they revolve centrally around the use and distribution of resources.

Hollick analyzes the likely consequences of current trends manifest in negotiations over the law of the seas. The erosion of an international commons governed by laissez faire norms through national "enclosure" of ocean space—the extension by riparian states of their jurisdictions over the continental shelf and economic zones—will create international problems when issues over navigation and communications conflict, as they are likely to, with national claims over the use of resources. Moreover, Hollick argues, uses by nations of their economic zones for purposes such as fishing and waste disposal are likely to affect neighbors seriously. For these and other reasons spelled out in her paper, Hollick sees current trends in negotiations over the oceans regime as unstable and undesirable. She proposes, as a long-term goal, a different type of regime, one designed not only to promote greater stability and certainty for governments in their uses of ocean space but also to satisfy efficiently what she calls "national concerns with dignity" and "equitable" material gain. Differing ideas about what is equitable are at the crux of international negotiations on resource management, and both the McCulloch-Piñera and Hollick studies offer views on how the quest for greater equity should be factored into international decisions affecting resources development and trade.

Although the three essays in this volume deal with different facets of the problem of resource management, they deal with three common themes. First, their analyses and prescriptions confront the issue of why the management of commodity trade has become a critical issue in relations between poor and rich societies. Second, their proposals focus upon the major problem of resource management at the international institutional level: how to create a system that provides for both an equitable distribution of scarce resources and, at the opposite end of the supply spectrum, an equitable adjustment when resources are abundant or even superabundant. Third, they each deal with questions about international processes for controlled change and, in particular, with means of creating practicable mechanisms through which the goals of resource management can be achieved. In the remaining pages of this introduction, each of these three clusters of issues will be spelled out in greater detail.

COMMODITIES AND THE DEVELOPING COUNTRIES

Many persons would argue that the attention developing countries have focused on national control over resources and on international intervention into commodity markets reflects their desire to find some means of creating, through extortion, a redistribution of wealth from rich to poor societies. Some would even maintain that these less developed countries (LDCs) are much less interested in changing trading rules in order to benefit their populations than they are in increasing their own international power and prestige at the expense of Western countries. These attitudes toward the developing world might be understandable in the context of efforts by some LDC governments to gain commodity power during the past few years. To be sure, these antipathetic orientations toward the North-South dialogue are based in many instances upon an unavoidable fact of life in some Third World countries: namely, their governments are corrupt, the structure of income distribution within them is unbalanced (with a small percentage of the population holding a disproportionately large share of wealth and a much larger group remaining absolutely as well as relatively impoverished), and their foreign policies are often aggressively pursued against the West as a means of diverting domestic attention away from those domestic problems that they have been unwilling or unable to address.

Others dissent from the approach taken by developing countries on more limited economic grounds. They assert that the approach would make even more difficult the process of adjustment through which developing countries must pass if they are to achieve their goals of industrialization. And they note that those developing countries most likely to benefit from the redistributional aspects of the approaches being suggested—the middle-income societies—are least in need of "international subsidization."

While these attitudes are attractive for many persons in the West, they grossly overstate the "demands" of developing countries and misconstrue the critical role played by commodities in the domestic politics of most LDCs. As McCulloch and Piñera note, commodity exports—if one includes oil—are responsible for about 80 percent of the export earnings of the developing countries. Excluding oil, the share of primary commodity exports of the non-oil exporting developing countries drops—but not to below 61%. So long as the structure of their exports remains heavily concentrated in primary products, their ability to achieve a wide spectrum of domestic goals is extraordinarily dependent upon the conditions of supply and demand in international markets over which no single developing country exercises much control—except perhaps in the case of Saudi Arabia and oil. That is to say, many LDC governments are highly vulnerable to prevailing conditions in international commodity markets which can almost capriciously wreak havoc with the domestic political stability of any single developing society.

Hard-currency export earnings provide the largest source of foreign exchange for the purchase of both capital goods and consumer goods. If the major goal of developing countries is rapid economic growth and industrialization—which require imports of capital goods—planning for growth is highly dependent upon export earnings. In this regard, what LDCs seek in a regulated international market is greater certainty about export earnings so that domestic economic plans can be implemented smoothly rather than in fits and starts. Similarly, if governments in most developing countries need the support of middle- and upper-class elite groups to maintain authority, they need to assure

7

that a stream of consumer goods can be imported to satisfy their politically most important constitutents.

Examples abound of developing country governments—or leaders—who lost power in part because international commodity markets severely affected domestic political stability. Perhaps the most notable example was Ghana's Nkrumah, whose government was overthrown in a coup d'état in 1966. Although his repressive policies and mismanagement had created widespread resentment against his regime, the immediate cause of his overthrow was the inability of his government to pay for his ambitious development projects. The government's international debt burden for these projects could not be serviced as a result of enormous shortfalls in export earnings caused by the plummeting price of cocoa, which accounted for over 60 percent of Ghana's exports.

Beyond these vulnerabilities to market fluctuations, which link LDC export earnings to cyclical fluctuations in the West, where the major customers are, and to supply conditions in other exporting countries, there are underlying structural conditions in the world economy that seem to be detrimental to many commodity exporters. Although the arguments here are somewhat contentious, there are strongly held beliefs in the developing world that, over the long run, the terms of trade adversely affect exporters of primary products and benefit exporters of industrial products. That is to say, despite large cyclical fluctuations, the prices of many primary products seem to have fallen over time in relation to the prices of the industrial goods that LDCs import, but this issue of the terms of trade is highly contentious. It is widely believed within LDCs that this structural condition in world economic relationships makes it increasingly costly and therefore more difficult for developing countries to industrialize.

In addition, therefore, to their desire to stabilize their export earnings, there is a widespread belief in the developing world that intervention into market conditions is required to change what appear to be adverse terms of trade. Price manipulation, it is believed, would enable LDCs to achieve this change and to increase earnings from exports of primary products.

A third aspect of the attention LDCs have drawn to commodity markets relates, in part, to a vague sense of national dignity and to a specific indignation against international trading rules that appear to be unjust and inequitable. Developing countries not only find themselves uniquely vulnerable to the uncertainties of market fluctuations and to steadily rising costs for imported capital goods, but they also see their exports unfairly and sometimes capriciously affected by the investment and import policies of the industrial West.

While 80 percent of LDC export earnings stem from primary products (including oil), the LDCs are not the only, or even the major, exporters of such products, since some of the world's primary industrial countries, such as the United States and the Soviet Union, are also major producers and exporters of primary products. The papers by Arad and Arad and by McCulloch and Piñera document the market competitiveness between developing and developed countries in specific commodities. In some instances, such developing country exports as cotton and semitropical fruits are often discriminated against by tariff and quota barriers. More important, LDCs face barriers to the markets of developed countries for semiprocessed and manufactured goods. So long as such barriers exist, developing countries fear that they will be unable to develop markets of a sufficient scale to make it economically worth their while. Their efforts to market semiprocessed and manufactured goods relate, of course, to the desire to increase export earnings and become more industrialized.

In short, developing countries find the rules governing international trade, which were laid down by the world's largest trading countries—those in the industrialized West—to be a major obstacle to their own industrialization and success in earning income from exports. Furthermore, they feel that unless they are able to industrialize, they will remain dependent upon the earnings they receive from primary products, which means vulnerability, impoverishment, and continued loss of dignity.

Given the salience of commodity issues in political and economic life in most developing countries, it is scarcely surprising that Southern states have focused upon commodity management in their efforts to change the rules of the international economic order. LDCs have been attracted both to arrangements to assure price stabilization and export-earnings stabilization in order to reduce the amplitude of cyclical fluctuations and to mechanisms to increase prices for their exports in order to enhance their earnings. Buffer-stock and compensatory finance arrangements and the type of insurance mechanism favored by McCulloch and Piñera are variants of proposals designed to create greater certainty in the international economic environment and therefore to make the environment for development planning and domestic politics more secure.

Some of the same factors that have focused LDCs' attention on international commodity markets have also increased their desire either to nationalize foreign investment in raw-materials industries or to change regulations concerning equity in order to assure that control over supply and income from raw-material production is in the hands of nationals. Although the trend toward nationalization seems to have slowed, considerable uncertainty surrounds issues of ownership of equity capital; and this uncertainty may be one key to the future of both the world supply of many raw materials and of the framework in which commodities are handled. For example, one result of this uncertainty has been a reluctance on the part of businesses in the industrial world to invest in the primary sector in LDCs, and this reluctance is likely to be reflected in future shortages in some areas by the mid-1980s. This example illustrates the growing mutuality of interest between rich and poor societies in the health of resource markets and the world economy as a whole.

Although the North-South dialogue has not yielded significant tangible results so far, it has generated at least this one positive result: the increased recognition in industrial Northern governments that it is desirable to inject greater certainty into the international trade arrangements upon which developing countries acutely depend. This perceptual change is likely to become more widespread in years to come. One reason, however, why tangible results have been less fruitful than many LDCs desire is that there is great uncertainty about *how* the international economic

environment can be made more secure for LDCs. It was recognized at an early stage, for example, that price stabilization
arrangements could have perverse effects on the flow of developing-country exports and that it was total income from exports
rather than price stabilization per se that should be the focus of
international negotiation. Even so, as McCulloch and Piñera
show, arrangements designed to enhance security have differential short-term and long-term effects, and the trade-offs between them must be weighed carefully. Thus, for example, even
compensatory finance and insurance schemes, which in the short
run could create the security of earnings and access to hard
currency that LDCs desire, might in the long run impede efforts
to develop new exports of manufactured products that would,
over the long term, better bolster efforts both to industrialize
more rapidly and to earn even more through exports.

The uncertainty about how to inject the greater security sought
by LDCs into the international economic system is perhaps more
pervasive when attention is focused upon a second LDC aim:
to change adversely declining terms of trade for commodity exports. This uncertainty relates in part to measures of the terms
of trade. Indeed, it can be argued that many LDC perceptions
are bound more in ideological assumptions than in empirical
analysis. While the terms of trade of some exports have declined,
and those of others, like oil, have clearly been reversed, it is hard
to generalize about the direction of change for all commodities.
Uncertainty exists as well when discussion shifts to prescriptions
and policy recommendations. Even if the argument is accepted
that there has been a continuing decline in the terms of trade of
most LDC exports of primary products, it is by no means clear
that efforts to reverse the decline would succeed in increasing
or even stabilizing LDC export earnings. Since such efforts
involve manipulation of prices—usually through an association of producers designed to limit the quantity of supplies
introduced into markets—they provoke market reactions by both
importers and other potential suppliers. The resulting use of
substitutes or the entry into the market of new suppliers can
serve to undermine the initial efforts to change the terms of
trade.

"EQUITY" AND "POWER" IN NORTH-SOUTH RELATIONS

If commodity issues involve fundamental problems that are confronted by most developing countries, it is clear to most of them that "solving" commodity issues alone will not solve these problems of development. What is at stake is not simply alleviating market uncertainties or declining terms of trade, but larger structural issues related to industrialization and economic growth, the enhancement of domestic political authority and of international status and dignity abroad. Commodity issues, in short, are linked to a wide spectrum of other issues.

At the simplest level, they are linked to wider international trade issues: LDC commodity exporters will not be able to break out of their underdeveloped status unless they change their economic structures and the types of goods they export. They will not be able to export processed and industrial goods until they industrialize. But with limited domestic markets, they will not be able to export processed goods unless they develop markets for them abroad. In spite of the recent success of some developing countries, such as Brazil, Mexico, Taiwan, Hong Kong, Singapore, and South Korea, in this regard, LDCs find themselves confronting innumerable obstacles to selling their industrial products abroad, in part because of import barriers imposed by the industrial countries. Breaking out of the cycle requires—among other things—the dismantling of those obstacles, which in the minds of many governments in the developing world requires a change in the rules of international exchange that at worst would not discriminate against LDCs and at best would discriminate in their favor. The attempt by LDCs in the 1960s to commit the industrial countries to adopt GSP—a Generalized System of Preferences—were part of this effort to move out of the cycle of underdevelopment, but the scheme has yielded disappointing results since the developed states have limited its application.

Commodity issues are linked not only to the general framework of international commercial rules but also to a number of other economic and political issues. For example, commodity export earnings are directly related to the size of some countries' external debt—and to their abilities to service it. That is why compensatory finance and other insurance arrangements are such important issues. In recent years, however, the main linkage question in the commodity area has related to the uses of commodity power and whether producer arrangements can be developed to manipulate market conditions in such a way as to force the industrial countries to yield to the developing countries on a number of issues at stake in international negotiations.

There is little doubt that the major reason why commodity power became the focus of attention of LDC bargaining strategies during the 1970s was the "demonstration effect" of the achievements of OPEC in quadrupling oil prices in 1973–1974, of the sudden redistribution in international wealth and power that seemed to be achieved, and of the use of the oil weapon by some Arab members of OPEC in order to pressure the United States government to use its leverage over Israel in bargaining over the Middle East conflict.

The essay by Arad and Arad is a systematic effort to identify the critical elements in commodity power and to assess whether OPEC's achievement during the past decade can be replicated by other producer cartels in the coming decade. Their analysis supports a growing consensus that oil was very much of an exception, but that it provided a model during the 1970s for conducting a Southern bargaining strategy in the North-South dialogue. In many ways, the oil model serves as the political key to understanding why the Southern strategy proceeded as it did during the past few years, for the oil model, were it applicable to other commodities, had the appearance par excellence to be the way for Southern states to exercise resource power.

The oil example had two initial effects on North-South politics. First, it provided a demonstration effect for other Southern countries and impelled them to organize stronger producer associations. Second, it placed OPEC in a central position among developing countries in their effort to maintain a united position in the so-called Group of 77 (G-77). Although most LDCs are importers and were therefore at least as adversely affected by oil-price increases as were the developed countries, they became politically tied to OPEC not only in the hope that LDC unity

13

would result in their gaining access to OPEC aid to offset the price increases but also because they needed OPEC support in order to pursue their own goals in the North-South dialogue. Meanwhile, Arab members of OPEC used the support they received from other LDCs to pursue their own united front strategy on a Middle East settlement. (In return, African members of the G-77 gained OPEC support for their position on southern Africa.)

In spite of these initial "successes" of commodity power, the Southern strategy now seems clearly to have failed. Why is this the case? Why was the effort to center a Southern strategy on commodity power so unsuccessful? The analysis by Arad and Arad provides a key to understanding this central question. They propose a set of categories to understand the nature of commodity power, based on their own understanding of the dynamics of OPEC. In particular, they focus on three dimensions of power: what they call the relative level of *scarcity*, the distribution of *supply and demand conditions* on world markets, and what they term the *essentiality* of the resource in question. Although some resources, such as chromium and grains, seem to share some of the characteristics of oil, Arad and Arad argue that the cluster of characteristics that defines oil's commodity power makes oil a notable exception.

Oil, for example, is distributed so unevenly among countries that it is virtually unique as a commodity whose supply can be reduced on world markets by major suppliers. Conditions of manipulated scarcity are directly related, then, to the distribution of supply and demand conditions on the world market and, in particular, to the fact that the United States has become the single largest importer of petroleum and Saudi Arabia the major residual supplier of oil. Moreover, and key to OPEC's oil power, petroleum is *essential*. Petroleum is basic to the working of the world economy as the major source of energy for industrial production and, at least in the short-term to middle-term future, competition with substitutes is limited. Finally, while almost no other resource has these characteristics, the ones that do are not favorable to developing-country demands for redistribution of global wealth. Chromium, for example, finds its major producers

in Rhodesia and the Soviet Union, and foods—mostly grains—
are supplied largely by Northern countries.

Arad and Arad's analysis suggests not only that the exercise
of commodity power is likely to be rather limited during the next
decade but also that the term is elusive and must be seen in a
dynamic context. Even the oil power of OPEC is likely to be
more constrained, since the particular mix of political and economic circumstances that made its exercise feasible in the 1970s
is likely to change in the 1980s, the anticipated tightness of
supply through the 1990s notwithstanding. For OPEC countries—the "new rich" states of international society—market
access to—and investment opportunities in—the industrial West
are likely to make the North less a target of conflictual politics
during the next decade and will also probably turn the attention
of OPEC members away from other developing countries whose
own needs will increasingly diverge from theirs. More generally,
what the essay by Arad and Arad suggests is that economic
power is itself elusive in a dynamic international environment.
If OPEC's use of economic power is one of the most salient
characteristics of international politics during the last decade,
another is the rapidity with which economic power shifted in the
world and, accompanying this shift, the equally dramatic changes
in the nature and meaning of economic power that occurred.

If one takes a broader look at economic power during the
period since World War II, what is most remarkable about it is
how quickly it passed from some societies to others and how
rapidly its meaning was transformed. At the beginning of the
period, it appeared that America's economic dominance would
be a fact of international life for the remainder of this century.
By the late 1960s, however, there was almost universal agreement
that America had moved into a period of irreversible economic
decline and was being challenged by a united Western Europe
and Japan for economic prowess. Some analysts even felt that
the age of power politics, based on military might, was changing
to a new age of civilianized economic power in which militarily
weak states such as Japan and non-nuclear states such as
Germany would hold the basic economic levers. OPEC's price

increases revealed, however, the weakness that characterized Japan and Western Europe in an age of manipulated scarcities in which their vulnerability to the cutting off of supplies from abroad increased. Perhaps in the next decade the conceptualization of economic power will return to ideas prominent in the 1960s—namely, that taken together, economic growth, the total size of GNP, and the degree to which one government could make others dependent upon it and it less vulnerable to others define the nature of economic power.

Regardless of how economic power develops during the next decade, even if developing countries are unable to exercise commodity power, there will remain some fundamental problems in the management of resources in international society. Not only would the sorts of market imperfections described by McCulloch and Piñera continue to make the distribution of wealth less equitable than it might be, but the commodity markets will themselves continue to have skewed distributional effects that many societies will find to be inequitable. It is important to recall that the attraction to LDCs of commodity power resided in the ends that such power was to serve. The economic end was and remains greater equity in the distribution of world wealth. The redistributive claims of developing countries from the outset of the North-South confrontation have been based on the inequity of the global distribution of wealth, with one-quarter of the world's population consuming three-quarters of its resources. To be sure, there have been arguments that many LDC governments have intentionally confused equity as it applies to individuals with equity among states and that income distribution within many developing countries is far more inequitable than income distribution among countries. Nevertheless, the creation of more equitable circumstances on both of these dimensions will remain a major international issue for the coming decade.

In looking at the equity issues, which pervade the three essays in this volume, a distinction should be drawn between what seems desirable from a global perspective, on the one hand, and from the perspectives of individual governments, on the other. As McCulloch and Piñera argue, from a global perspective the resource issues relate to the need to assure an adequate supply and distribution of resources for equitable economic growth in the world; that is to say, in a growing international economy, developing-country growth should be somewhat higher than developed-country growth. In this regard, these two authors seek to find reasonable and equitable mechanisms and rules through which both scarce goods and superabundant goods can be allocated, that is, rules that are fair to all parties and that are seen as providing mutual benefits. The rules for equitable resource management would also apply to resources discussed by Hollick in her essay, namely, those in the seabeds—and by extension in Antarctica—which are not yet scarce but someday might be. These global perspectives differ with, and sometimes contradict, the perspectives through which individual governments regard resources. On this individual level, the problem is to find ways to assure low prices and adequate supply for consumption and high income for suppliers.

The task of finding equitable rules is by no means easy. Not only will it be difficult to make a global or world-order perspective predominate over individual national interests, but it will also be hard to find acceptable means to reconcile the perspectives held by individual governments when they contradict one another. It will also be difficult to find means to smooth out the market imperfections on both the demand and supply sides that McCulloch and Piñera have described. These incompatibilities and contradictions in approaches that need to be overcome might be summarized as follows:

- There are contradictions, noted earlier, between global and individual governmental perspectives on resource management.
- Anti-inflationary goals pursued by consuming countries are likely to contradict the goals of suppliers to receive the highest possible prices for their exports.
- Anti-inflationary goals of consumer countries also might well contradict other goals that they will pursue, including their objective to maintain uninterrupted supplies of commodity imports.
- Tensions will continue between the desire by commodity ex-

porters to wield commodity power and their desire to stabilize their earnings, when high prices do not necessarily assure a continuous flow of high export earnings.

- Efforts to regulate commodity trade in order to make it less unstable will contravene other trade and development issues, including the goal of diversifying and balancing LDC economies.

However difficult it might be to reconcile these and other problems confronted by governments in the management of resources, the quest for more equitable arrangements will be a central focus of international political life during the next decade. And even if perfect or ideal solutions are elusive, the quest will be driven by the overwhelming sense of inequity that characterizes the perceptions of most developing countries about commodity issues.

INTERNATIONAL INSTITUTIONAL REFORM

The reconciliation of differences between individual national perspectives and global perspectives on issues related to access to, and distribution of, resources requires international institutional reform. The search for better and new institutions is also driven by a factor singled out by Hollick in her analysis of the management of ocean space: the desire of most developing countries to enhance their national dignity by participating directly in the formulation and implementation of international policies that affect them. However, it is one thing to desire international institutional reform and another to develop new international mechanisms.

Many of the dilemmas of institutional design or reform are adumbrated in Hollick's essay. Unlike the problem of resource management in areas of commodity trade, in ocean space these dilemmas relate to designing a system that would provide equitable arrangements for the sharing of resources of the deep seabeds—an area neither under national jurisdiction nor in short supply as yet—and that have to date been technically accessible to no one but legally accessible to all societies. Hollick's preferred regime for the management of ocean space is one in which property rights are jointly owned by the governments of the world. But as Hollick demonstrates, present trends in the Third United Nations Conference on the Law of the Seas (UNCLOS III) move away from, rather than toward, such a preferred regime. The Conference is not likely to achieve an optimal—or even a decent—set of principles for managing fisheries, navigation, or environmental protection. It will benefit some—namely, the larger riparian states—far more than others, especially the developing countries. And if Hollick feels that the most troublesome aspect of these negotiations is their failure to provide security, almost as troublesome to her is the issue of national dignity.

The negotiations over a new regime to manage the oceans reflect problems that are inevitably encountered when a management system is designed: to be global (involving most, if not all, members of the UN system); to enhance participation by the rule of equality (one state, one vote); and to deal with a set of issues holistically (fisheries, navigation and shipping, deep-sea mining, and environmental protection). The quest for national dignity, which has been translated into the notion that each state has an equal right to participate in rule making and rule application, results in inefficiency and disorder and therefore might actually impede its achievement. As Hollick shows, in negotiations over economic zones and territorial waters in UNCLOS III, the end result of LDC efforts to preserve and enhance national dignity has been the skewing of economic benefits in favor of developed rather than developing countries.

Irrational results such as those that seem to be emerging from UNCLOS III are not the only, or even the primary, cost of overemphasizing universal participation as a means of satisfying the drive for national dignity. More significant, perhaps, is the slow process of rule making associated with global forums whose decision rules are based on one state, one vote. If the process of rule making can be slowed down by frequent deadlocks and difficult negotiations, the process of rule application is virtually impossible on this basis.

Fortunately, the effort to achieve a new oceans regime is not representative of desirable and necessary institutional reform in areas associated with resource management. It has been noted that UNCLOS III has been global in scope and open to universal participation because the issues related to the management of ocean space have been perceived to be global in nature. Other modes of rule making and rule application exist that can supplement or replace the rule of one state, one vote. These two processes, for example, can be separated into different "chambers" with a rule-making body assuring global participation and a rule-application body based on a process of selective membership, including "representation" membership. Or the principle of representation can apply to both. The Conference on International Economic Cooperation (CIEC)—the North-South dialogue—held in Paris from 1975 to 1977 was based on this sort of representational scheme, with some key nations participating on their own behalf and other governments representing the interest of wider groups. But the principle also created resentment on the part of those represented by others.

In most areas, however, there is no reason why participation needs to be global and universal. In the commodities area, forums for negotiations can be much more selective and based on principles of inclusion that would involve only the most important producing and consuming countries. All three of the essays in this volume implicitly or explicitly advocate management on less than universal bases. There are a number of arguments that can be made in favor of the development of different frameworks for negotiations for each commodity. The efficiency of smaller groups is an important, but by no means the only, argument that can be made for selective participation. Another is that the framework for negotiations should reflect the particular characteristics of the issue at stake. A framework for managing international fisheries, for example, ought to have a radically different membership and a different set of operating principles from one designed to manage copper or food supplies.

As McCulloch and Piñera argue, perhaps even more important is the ability of producing and exporting countries to find improved means to market their products so as to reap the benefits of efficiency and enhance security by selective membership. This suggests that a dual process should be at work. On the one hand, the network of LDC producers involved in supplying world markets—even if they compete with suppliers from the developed world—could well be strengthened by producer associations that had as a goal the improvement of the marketing capabilities of the members. On the other hand, if the most important producing and consuming countries would meet to improve market security, market efficiency could be further enhanced; at the same time, the perceived needs for direct participation and the goal of security could also be satisfied.

The growing interdependence between producers and consumers of different raw materials and other commodities indicates that it would be in the interests of both to achieve secured production and marketing arrangements. If, in the interest of assuring greater certainty of supply, the governments of the developed countries encourage the growth of certain forms of producer associations for marketing purposes and show a willingness to cooperate on assuring producers the security they seek in market access to the developed world and in a steady stream of export-generated income, the workings of sets of accommodations between suppliers and consumers could be in hand.

There are a number of benefits, then, that could be derived from establishing a multitude of frameworks for marketing different commodities. If greater efficiency is introduced into world markets as a result, other, more marginal, producing and consuming countries would also benefit. On the other hand, selective arrangements bring potential costs as well. These costs are essentially political and would be borne by societies that are not immediate participants in whatever arrangements are worked out. Nonparticipants would almost inevitably be affected by decisions made by those who do work out the new arrangements. They would, in short, bear the distributional costs that would accompany those arrangements, just as they would derive distributional benefits. However, they would do so without any direct say in rule application. Another political cost would affect the Group of 77 as a whole. The negotiation of arrangements on a commodity-by-commodity basis could well be viewed as an effort by developed countries to divide the G-77 and thereby to reduce its effectiveness as a political bargaining instrument. Developing countries have wanted to maintain a unified institutional forum for all commodity arrangements as a means of bolstering their overall impact. If the United Nations Conference on Trade and Development (UNCTAD) Secretariat were to have an overall monitoring function over the workings of all commodity arrangements, the LDCs' perceived needs in this area might be safeguarded. But it is hard to imagine a body that could efficiently serve as a forum for negotiation over all commodity arrangements unless it were to be a part of a much revised international trade institution.

Many other institutional questions can be added to the list of those already covered. In particular, there is a range of questions that arise over the nature and pace of institutional change. These questions have both theoretical and practical political importance. Some persons have argued, especially when they have the Malthusian perspective outlined by Arad and Arad, that the world has become so interdependent that institutional reform concerned with the allocation of increasingly scarce resources not only must come at once, but also must relate everything to everything else. Others argue against this position, not simply because they deem the Malthusian argument wrong, but also because they fear that linking together many issues in a single body will lead to inefficiency and political stalemate. Moreover, they feel that the world has not become so interdependent as to make this sort of linkage necessary, but that doing so will interrelate phenomena that should be kept separate so that issues and processes can be buffered from one another. These larger institutional questions are treated elsewhere in the 1980s Project and in many ways are more important for a time horizon that is longer than that of the essays that appear in this volume.

Scarce Natural Resources and Potential Conflict

Ruth W. Arad and Uzi B. Arad

ONE

Introduction

This study is primarily an attempt to examine where and under what conditions armed conflicts over the control of—and access to—scarce natural resources are likely to occur in the late 1980s. Given the economic and political dislocations that occurred in the aftermath of the Arab oil embargo and the fourfold increase in the price of crude oil imposed by OPEC a few years ago, the present concern about the state of the earth's resources needs no explanation.

The focus of this paper will be on the macro level. On the micro level of international politics, speculations about the future are bound to be fallible: leaders and regimes will come and go, and issues will wax and wane in importance. The only thing one can say with any degree of certainty about the political scene of the 1980s is that it will be different from today's.

Equally fallible will be conjectures about conflicts and disputes on the micro level, such as those between neighboring states. The sheer number of permutations would make any attempt to list the possibilities pointless. Furthermore, the micro level, by definition, involves problems on a lesser order of magnitude that are, consequently, less critical to identify as far in advance as problems on the macro level. Indeed, macro-level phenomena, apart from being more important to speculate about, are more susceptible to a forward-looking analysis. In drawing a picture of the future, the broad outlines are less likely to be in error than the lesser details.

From a macro-level perspective, three types of confrontation on the political side of the politics-resources nexus warrant our attention. Two are global in scope—the conflict between the developing and the developed groups of countries, i.e., North versus South; the rivalry between the superpowers, i.e., East versus West—and the third, regional—the tension between neighboring countries or hegemonic powers and surrounding countries in a sort of South versus South confrontation. It is in relation to these three types of confrontation that the question of the role of natural resources will be posed. Although much depends on political developments within these three axes of contention, it is sufficient, for discussion purposes, to realize that all three are certain—if anything at all can be said to be certain—to persist.

Assessing the future condition of raw materials is somewhat easier. This is so because in the area of resource economics a discussion with a temporal horizon of 10 years or so is not really a futuristic endeavor. The reason is plain enough: with lead times averaging 5 to 10 years, the resource world of the 1980s has already been largely determined by economic plans, investment decisions, and similar steps already taken or soon to be.[1] In other words, to use present assessments as a starting point in this discussion, rather than to disengage from them entirely in order to conjecture about what might be true in the 1980s, would not be so gross a distortion as it might be were the subject of this essay more mutable.

In the following discussion, we will first consider those nonrenewable resources that might endow Third World producers with a political instrument; then attempt to pinpoint locations on the globe whose expected geostrategic significance—because of the presence of valuable resources—might attract the attention of the superpowers, thus precipitating a confrontation; and finally, assess the likelihood that hegemonial powers will intervene to gain access to resources.

[1]The relative short-term nonmanipulability of resource policies is discussed by Nazli Choucri and Robert C. North in their "Dynamics of International Conflicts: Some Policy Implications of Population, Resources and Technology," in Raymond Tanter and Richard H. Ullman (eds.), *Theory and Policy in International Relations*, Princeton University Press, Princeton, N.J., 1972, p. 89.

TWO

North-South: The Mobilization of Resource Power

There is indeed a very real and growing threat from the Third World unless the industrialized countries, particularly the United States, both stand up to the producer cartels and begin to adopt far more cooperative policies toward them . . . . In fact, producer cartels look more feasible in other commodities than in oil. . . . I continue to fear that oil is only the beginning.[2]

NORTH-SOUTH CONFLICT AND RESOURCE POWER

The quotation above from C. Fred Bergsten's famous 1974 article in *Foreign Policy* deserves our attention. It implies, in the first place, that the political—not just the commercial—balance of power has recently been changing in the Third World's favor and, in the second place, that the sensible thing for the advanced, industrialized countries to do would be to better adapt themselves to the changing circumstances by simultaneously "standing up" to the cartels and turning "far more cooperative" toward them.

The prescriptive element here obviously depends upon the validity of the predictive one, for nothing could be more pathetic than to adopt Bergsten's policy recommendation only to learn that the threat he warned about turned out to be bogus. It is therefore important that we initially address ourselves to an ex-

[2]C. Fred Bergsten, "The Threat Is Real," *Foreign Policy*, no. 14, 1974, pp. 84–90. See also the same author's "The Threat from the Third World," *Foreign Policy*, no. 11, 1973, pp. 102–124.

amination of Bergsten's predictive premise, leaving aside his prescriptive note for later consideration. In examining this premise, however, we should not look at the problem from the view that other cartels are likely to follow in the steps of OPEC. Rather, we should take the more general politico-economic perspective of Bergsten and analyze whether raw materials are indeed being turned by the less developed countries (LDCs) into new and effective political instruments of influence to be used to enhance their position and advance their economic and political claims vis-à-vis the industrialized world.

Admittedly, the challenge of the spectacularly successful Organization of Petroleum Exporting Countries and the Organization of Arab Petroleum Exporting Countries (OPEC/OAPEC) to the industrial countries of the noncommunist bloc seemed, to quite a few observers, to herald the dawn of a new era in North-South relations. The balance of power between the two camps, they argued, was gradually changing in favor of the developing countries, with power, influence, and the determination to use them shifting away from the developed, industrial nations. This process, continued the observers, had its roots in the fundamental asymmetry between the two camps. For although the developing countries scarcely control all the world's raw-material reserves, they do, by virtue of their industrial backwardness and their consequent lesser need for such resources, have a surplus of them. In contrast, the developed countries, more often than not, are in a resource deficit precisely because of their allegedly insatiable demand for raw materials, a demand that simply reflects their being at a more advanced stage of industrialization.[3]

Northern dependence on Southern exports of raw materials is potentially transformable into actual political leverage for two reasons. First, the industrialized countries' need for raw materials imported from the developing world renders them sensitive to the political and economic pressures from the South; this

---

[3]For a description of this process from a point of view sympathetic to exporters of raw materials, see Zuhayr Mikdashi's *The International Politics of Natural Resources*, Cornell University Press, Ithaca, N.Y., 1976.

vulnerability is counterbalanced by the developing countries' dependence on their export earnings as well as on imports from the developed world.[4] Second, in an age of nuclear stalemate and a growing emphasis on the pursuit of economic—rather than security—interests by the developed countries, the relative significance of international economic relations has increased. Power politics revolving around such relations has grown in importance, paralleled by a decline in the utility attached to conventional power politics conducted from a military power base. This has brought about a weakening of the overall Northern posture vis-à-vis the South, with the North's military advantage being eroded as a viable political instrument.

That the North still represents a group of dominant nations, both in economic and in military terms, is evident. On the other hand, its growing deficit of raw materials appears to give the militarily inferior Southern countries an employable economic weapon. Although a growing resource dependence on the South will not necessarily mean that the balance has been decisively tipped against the North, it may mean that there is a higher probability that states of the North will use force to assure access to resources in times of stress.

In abstract terms, if countries from each of the camps are ever to approach the brink of war, they might well follow a two-stage process. The first would have to involve a successful manipulation by the less developed country, or group of countries, of its control over strategic natural resources required by the North. The second stage, coming as a reaction to the first, might involve a military response by those developed countries most threatened, or otherwise adversely affected, by such resource manipulation.

This simple model of a two-stage escalation suggests that the occurrence of war under such circumstances would come—if at all—only as a direct consequence of an effective venture in economic warfare by the South. The question that arises in as-

---

[4]Robert O. Keohane and Joseph S. Nye provide in their *Power and Interdependence* (Little, Brown & Co., Boston, 1977) a thoughtful discussion of the political and economic effects of complex interdependencies.

sessing the likelihood of such a hypothetical escalation is whether sufficient political power inheres in the ownership of natural resources, such that their use by the South in waging effective economic warfare—that is, by threatening the "strangulation" of Northern economies—impels the North to react militarily.

In more ways than one, OPEC can hardly be considered either unique or ephemeral. The cartelization and politicization of the petroleum market gave a noticeable impetus to a more general Southern onslaught against the present economic order, particularly as the OPEC challenge to the most powerful nations of the West was seen to elicit a rather supine response. Thus, as OPEC was "scoring points," other resource exporters were trying to emulate it and even formally codified their right to do so. In 1973, the UN's Economic and Social Committee issued a resolution saying that it

recognizes that one of the most effective ways in which the developing countries can protect their natural resources is to promote or strengthen machinery for cooperation among them, having as its main purpose to concert pricing policies, to improve conditions of access to markets, to coordinate production policies and, thus, to guarantee the full exercise of sovereignty by developing countries over their natural resources.[5]

A year later, subsumed within the general platform calling for the establishment of a New Economic Order, the UN General Assembly strongly supported the formation of producer-exporter associations. In 1975, at the Dakar Conference of Developing Countries on Raw Materials, the Third World countries set up the mechanisms for governmental consultation and cooperation among these associations. Since then, every nonaligned countries' conference or Third World meeting has reiterated their need to form commodity groupings in order to improve not only their economic welfare but their political standing as well.[6]

The question of whether resources as such offer the political

[5]Cited by Mikdashi, op. cit., p. 196.

[6]The most important document in this connection is the Declaration on the Establishment of a New International Economic Order, UN General Assembly

leverage that Third World countries—properly organized—hope to derive from them is closely related to the currently popular study of the potential for commodity cartels in the future. In both instances the question is, How likely is a group of countries to dominate a certain market? But there is a difference. Our search is not for the equivalents of OPEC, for that organization seems bent on maximizing its *commercial* or *economic* returns. The real threat, to use Bergsten's admonition, lies with OAPECs of the future. It is the latter organization, having the avowed goal of maximizing the joint *political* returns for its members, which has already actively engaged in open economic warfare when it stopped selling oil to certain countries in 1973. The two types of organizations, though they partly overlap, should not be confused. Our interest is not in cartels that merely try to improve the terms of trade, but rather in politico-economic alliances that have the potential power, through the cartelization of a market, to attain political objectives.

Seen this way, it becomes clear that political influence does not automatically accrue through mere possession by a nation or group of nations of any industrial raw material. A number of prerequisite conditions—what may, in fact, be a somewhat rare combination of them—need to exist simultaneously in order for a raw material to endow those who control its supply with any political benefits. Specifically, three such sets of conditions need to apply. The first set, *scarcity*, pertains to the global, physical availability of the raw material in question, relative to other natural resources as well as possible substitutes. The second set of conditions, *distribution*, is concerned with the political and economic character of the market for the specific raw material, its existence in reserve form among the consuming nations, and its pattern of consumption. The third set, *essentiality*, relates to the intrinsic importance of the raw material under examination either in security or in economic terms. Together these conditions constitute the prerequisites for resource power.

Resolution 3201 (S-VI), May 1, 1974. The Dakar Declaration of the Conference of Developing Countries on Raw Materials (February 3–8, 1975) was reprinted as UNCTAD Document TD/B/C.1/L.45.

PREREQUISITES FOR RESOURCE POWER

Scarcity

The belief that an intensification of international disputes over resources is likely to occur sometime in the foreseeable future is partly predicated on the assumption that the political value of a raw material, not unlike its economic value as manifested in its price, is inversely related to its general availability. Implicit in this belief is a second underlying assumption that at present rates of consumption, many natural resources will soon be depleted, or nearly so.

Concern over the limits of our resources, as was noted at the outset, is rather commonplace today. Moreover, there have been quite a few attempts to have the limits estimated with some precision. Yet the process of estimation remains inexact, and there are still too many discrepancies among the various estimates found in the relevant literature. Much as they may differ, however, about both the methods of estimation and the results when applied over the long run, most experts do concur about the short run (which we define to be the next decade) and also tend to agree on the medium run (i.e., the next two). Typical of that body of opinion is the statement made by a team of experts assembled by the Brookings Institution:

We can flatly rule out lasting *real and radical shortages* for the rest of this century—that is, an outright exhaustion of resources in contrast to a situation in which demand temporarily outstrips supply. Neither for the minerals nor for renewable commodities is there any likelihood that physical constraints in this sense will operate over the next quarter century or for a decade or two beyond.[7]

[7]Kenzo Hemmi et al., *Trade in Primary Commodities: Conflict on Cooperation*, The Brookings Institution, Washington, D.C., 1974, p. 23. Other sources for estimates of availability include the Preliminary Papers of the 1st World Symposium on Energy and Raw Materials, held in Paris, June 6–8, 1974; the collection of articles in the Annals of the American Academy of Political and Social Science entitled *Adjusting to Scarcity*, Philadelphia, July 1975; and Wassily Leontief's UN report, *The Future of the World Economy*, Oxford University Press, New York, 1977.

So much for the prevalent popular fear that the world is on the verge of reaching the point of "systemic overload" and collapse due to the exhaustion of vital materials. It should, nonetheless, be noted that such a mood in itself *could* breed the same grave political difficulties caused by real—not imaginary—scarcities. Furthermore, while radical and lasting shortages are indeed not expected before the turn of the century, it is possible that certain resources will either approach exhaustion or exhibit greater supply sensitivity than others.

Resources whose supply might be—or might be perceived to be—tight two decades hence are thus bound to gain in political significance by the 1980s. Before scanning the entire range of materials in search for those that might present supply problems, a methodological note is in order.

First, although a plethora of assessments of the earth's mineral endowment exists, many of the discrepancies among them are due to the absence of a universally accepted, standard terminology with respect to the main variables. A second problem is that, even where the technical and terminological categorization is similar, methodological differences in the processes of estimation and forecasting often result in widely discrepant results. Third, there is not one single survey of the global availability of resources that is, at the same time, methodologically appropriate, current in its data base, and exhaustive in its coverage of the range of relevant resources.

The most critical point that needs to be made in connection with the first of these problems is that an estimate of reserves does *not* indicate the real extent of the geological availability of a certain mineral in the earth's crust. All it provides is an educated guess about the amount of the resource that analysis (or geological and engineering data) says should exist under current economic and operating conditions.

It is necessary, therefore, to add to this figure two other numbers—that which represents the amount known to exist but uneconomic to produce, and another number for the amount of undiscovered material, which may, or may not, be economic to produce. The McKelvey classification, used by the U.S. Bureau of Mines and the Geological Survey, calls the former category

33

"identified resources" and the latter "undiscovered resources." The category of undiscovered resources is further subdivided—according to the degree of certainty—into "hypothetical" and "speculative" subcategories.[8] It should be realized, however, that even these figures do not actually provide an estimate of ultimate resources. Table 1 presents estimates for each resource.

One thing should be clear, then: present techniques of estimating reserves do not assist us in measuring the relative scarcity of resources. The *concept* of reserves, to be sure, is in extensive use among industrial and governmental circles, for it is useful as an accounting concept, but it is not relevant in gauging the true physical availability of a resource, since all it does is provide us with the size of the inventory—man-made stocks—of that resource. To confuse an estimate of the proved reserves of a resource with its total availability would be quite misleading.

Absolute figures of mineral endowment do not convey very much in and of themselves. They have to be related to figures of current and expected consumption, since absolute figures of availability are meaningless unless measured against both present and future demand for them. The relevant yardstick to convey that relationship is that of the "life span"—the time to exhaustion—of each resource, which can be obtained by calculating the number of years of consumption provided by a given stock of the mineral.[9] Such figures are available in the literature, and only by contrasting total resources with the schedule of expected future consumption can we obtain a standardized estimate of a mineral's life span.

In strict economic terms it would be correct to reject such life-span calculations and to claim, as Houthakker has, that "the

[8]The McKelvey classification is not universally used. J. T. S. Govett and M. H. Govett, in their "The Concept and Measurement of Mineral Reserves and Resources" (*Resources Policy*, vol. 1, no. 1, September 1974, pp. 46–55), proposed another classification, which is intended to be more sensitive to the grades of minerals. Another useful discussion of the measurement problem is provided in W. V. Engelhardt, "Resources and Reserves of Metals," *Resources Policy*, vol. 1, no. 4, June 1975, pp. 186–191.

[9]For a discussion of such formulae see W. v. Engelhardt, op. cit., p. 188, and F. E. Banks, "Natural Resource Availability: Some Economic Aspects," *Resources Policy*, vol. 3, no. 1, March 1977, pp. 10–11.

world will never run out of any nonrenewable resource provided prices are allowed to adjust."[10] Yet there is some heuristic value in assessing the future availability of resources using life-span estimates, even if one uses the smaller reserves figure as a base. First, such estimates do provide an indication of the relative abundance of a given resource. Second, life-span figures *do* affect people's thinking and attitudes. Policy-makers tend to look at life-span figures, and such figures are regularly used in public discourse. As such, they constitute an input into the political decision-making process. The faulty economic logic underlying them is politically immaterial, and Houthakker himself readily admits that the point he made is widely ignored.

Having said that, it is now possible to move on to an examination of life-span figures armed with the assumption that the potential political influence associated with availability is best conveyed by comparing life spans. Clearly, a potentially alarming situation would exist were we to find a critical mineral whose life span does not stretch, say, for more than a decade. Control over such a resource would certainly provide one with a powerful instrument of influence throughout that crucial period. At the same time, such power would make its possessors potential targets of aggression, but more about that below.

Table 2 shows life-span figures for various resources as estimated separately by four analysts. Of the 15 minerals listed, 5 stand out with respect to scarcity: petroleum, zinc, tin, lead, and copper.[11] However, *only* if we assume that prices will remain constant or even decline should we be concerned with the state of these resources. It is evident that as prices rise, more and more of the currently subeconomic resources that are known to

[10]Hendrik S. Houthakker, "The Economics of Non-renewable Resources," Discussion Paper No. 493, Harvard Institute of Economic Research, Cambridge, Mass., July 1976, p. 10.

[11]Wassily Leontief and his associates, in a study conducted for the UN, utilized a somewhat different approach to measure the adequacy of resources. Relying upon a global economic model of the world economy and a rather conservative scenario, they found that only lead and zinc could be expected to "run out" by the turn of the century. Once the conservative assumptions were relaxed, they concluded that the world's resources of metallic minerals and fossil fuels are generally sufficient to supply world requirements through

TABLE 1
Estimates of World Mineral Endowment (in 10⁶ Tons)

	(1) Economic Reserves	(2) Identified but Un-economic Resources	(3) Undiscovered (Hypothetical and Speculative) Resources	(4) (2) + (3)
Nonferrous				
Aluminum (bauxite)	3,600	—	—	potential resources huge
Copper	370	750	720	1,470
Lead	144	1,644	210	1,854
Tin	4.7	22.4	18.8	41.2
Zinc	131	1,655	3,941	5,606
Ferrous and Ferro-alloys				
Iron	97	253	—	—
Chromium	466	1,215	1,008	2,223
Cobalt	2.7	4.5	—	—
Manganese	2,437	5,325	3,750	9,075
Molybdenum	4.7	31.5	1,100	—
Nickel	46	70	—	—

Fossil Fuels

Coal, all ranks*	1,400	9,500	7,300	16,800
Petroleum†	625	—	—	7,700
Tar sands†	—	—	—	915
Oil shale†	—	3,098	9,250	12,348
Natural gas‡	1,897	—	—	24,275

Nuclear Fuels

Uranium		1.1	3.3	4.4
Thorium		0.4	2.3	2.7

*In 10^9 tons.
†In 10^9 barrels.
‡In 10^{12} cubic feet.

SOURCE: Adapted from Indira Rajaraman, "Non-Renewable Resources: A Review of Long-Term Projections," *Futures*, June 1976, p. 237.

TABLE 2
Alternative Life-Span Figures of World Resource Endowment (in Years)

	Economic Reserves				Identified but Uneconomic Resources	Total Resources		
	CIEP's Estimate* (1)	Rajaraman's Estimate (2)	Banks's Estimate (3)	Engelhardt's Estimate (4)	Rajaraman's Estimate (5)	Rajaraman's Estimate (6)	Banks's Estimate (7)	MacGregor's Estimate* (8)
Nonferrous								
Aluminum (bauxite)	B	43–56	—	31	—	—	—	F
Copper	A	29	30.6	21	43	59	63.3	E
Lead	A	26–29	35.5	21	93–132	97–139	131.5	D
Tin	A	14–18	19.3	—	49–80	70–141	87.7	D
Zinc	A	15	20.3	18	65	97	123.3	D
Ferrous and Ferro-alloys								
Iron	C	57	56	93	80	—	—	E
Chromium	C	70–94	85	95	97–138	115–167	225	D
Cobalt	C	56–74	62	—	69–104	—	—	B
Manganese	B	17–96	77	46	93–121	—	—	E
Molybdenum	C	26–29	—	34	59–72	—	—	D
Nickel	C	32–39	35	53	40–50	—	—	D

	A	B	C	D	E	F
Fossil Fuels						
Coal, all ranks	—	73	—	131	—	—
Petroleum	—	20	—	—	63	—
Nuclear fuels						
Uranium	—	—	—	17	29	—
Thorium	—	—	—	—	—	—

*A, less than 25 years; B. 26 to 50 years; C, 51 to 100 years; D, 101 to 200 years; E, 201 to 400 years; F, more than 400 years. SOURCES: Adapted from the Council on International Economic Policy's *Special Report: Critical Imported Materials*, Washington, D.C., December 1974; Indira Rajaraman's "Non-Renewable Resources," *Futures*, vol. 8, June 1976; F. E. Banks's "Natural Resource Availability: Some Economic Aspects," *Resources Policy*, vol. 3, no. 1, March 1977; W. v. Engelhardt's "Resources and Reserves of Metals," *Resources Policy*, vol. 1, no. 4, June 1975; Ian D. MacGregor's "Natural Distribution of Metals and Some Economic Effects," American Academy of Political and Social Science Annals, vol. 420, 1975.

exist will become commercially attractive to produce. As column 5 in Table 2 demonstrates, the known deposits of these resources, though not yet economic, are quite large. Uranium, apparently, remains the most restricted, followed by copper, zinc, and oil. Still, price increases, depending on specific price elasticities, will tend to prolong time to exhaustion by simultaneously moderating consumption and increasing the total amount of economic reserves.[12] Higher prices would also encourage exploration, thereby shifting resources from the "undiscovered" category to the "identified," and possibly even to the "economic." The figures for total resources given in Table 2 suggest, then, that no single resource, except uranium, will even approach its half-life point by the end of the century. The relative tightness of supply of petroleum, copper, zinc, and tin is primarily an issue of price as far as the short run is concerned.

There is another factor that could mitigate the actual long-term threat of physical shortage of the resources discussed here. None of these particular resources is acutely lacking in possible substitutes, although, with the possible exception of lead, substitution may be encumbered by technological or financial difficulties. Copper can be replaced in many of its uses by other available materials, but such substitution may require high initial investment and new equipment. Lead, which may be in moderately tight supply in the future, is not easily replaceable; for most current uses of lead, there are simply no substitutes. Large-scale recycling, however, is possible. Zinc, on the other hand,

the remaining decades of this century and probably into the early part of the next century as well. Leontief, however, hastens to add that this conclusion does not necessarily preclude the occurrence of regional shortages and/or price increases. For details about the model and other pertinent observations see *The Future of the World Economy*, pp. 44–48.

[12]Data about elasticities show that while there usually cannot be much short-run reaction to changes in the price of several of the most important minerals, in the long run they may be rather significant. J. Herin and P. M. Wijkman, in their *Den Internationella Bakgrunden*, Langtidsutredringen, 1975 Stockholm 1976 (quoted by F. E. Banks, op. cit., p. 7), give the following price elasticities: copper—short run, 0.2, long run 2.50; tin—short run, 0.55, long run, 1.25; zinc—short run, 0.23.

does have many potential surrogates for its metallic uses, with lag time in shifting to them being only a year. There is, however, no substitute for it in its chemical use in vulcanizing rubber. Finally, there are numerous potential substitutes for most uses of petroleum as an energy source, but they could hardly replace oil in quantity. Furthermore, such substitution is very price-dependent and requires substantial time for shifting and retooling.[13] It is a fortunate quirk of nature that the two least replaceable materials, chromium and platinum, are available in rather large quantities.

In sum, quite a few resources may be in potentially tight supply by the end of the century. Of these, the most sensitive seem to be petroleum, lead, zinc, and copper. Other resources whose availability may be problematic include mercury, tungsten, uranium, and natural gas. Nevertheless, most of these resources often have substitutes for their major uses, and their total availability is large. The expected tight-supply situation, therefore, is more likely to result in price increases, followed by reduced demand and increased substitution, rather than in real physical shortages. Higher prices for these resources, however, hardly imply increased political leverage, as that ultimately depends on other attributes of the resource in question—its global distribution and its essentiality as a raw material.

Distribution

That a certain resource is in potentially tight supply is not sufficient to establish it as an effective political power base. What is also necessary, as is true in all instances where power and influence are used, is for a definite asymmetry to prevail with respect to that particular resource such that a power gradient develops. This asymmetry can arise if, and only if, supply and

[13]For a description and analysis of 19 key commodities, including their principal uses, market structure, and expected demand and supply trends through 1980, see the Council on International Economic Policy's *Special Report: Critical Imported Materials*, Washington, D.C., December 1974, pp. A-1–A-61.

demand become differentially distributed among the world's nations. Our concern here, however, is not with the general potential for monopolistic control of raw materials. Rather, it is confined to an examination of the North-South balance in resource power. Our task is to find those instances of asymmetry in which supply and export capabilities are concentrated in the hands of a few developing countries that need to deal with a multitude of industrialized, consumer nations. (The opposite case, that of monopsonic power, does, of course, affect market conditions, but it is less relevant to the resource-power relationship as it is discussed here).

The diffusion of export potential has the effect of curtailing the political power associated with it, just as the diffusion of import potential usually enhances it. The "ideal" asymmetry discussed here, and that which is bound to generate great political leverage, concerns a commodity whose supply is highly concentrated and whose import-demand is nearly universal. In order to examine the existence of such conditions, we should consult two scatter functions: that of supply and that of demand. The relevant parameters for both functions are those measuring and conveying degrees of dependence, for it is the precise nature of the balance of interdependence between the industrialized, importing countries and the developing, exporting countries that will determine the consequent resource-power relationship. Table 3 lists, in percentage form, the current degree of import-dependence of the three main groups in the industrialized, noncommunist world.

Table 3 shows that, of the materials surveyed, some seven present varying degrees of universal Northern dependence on imports. These are, roughly in descending order of import-dependence, chromium, tin, cobalt, nickel, petroleum, manganese, and bauxite. The fact that the United States, Western Europe, and Japan are heavily dependent upon these resources does not necessarily imply that Southern countries control the movement of these resources; the chromium supply, for instance, is controlled by South Africa and Rhodesia; nickel is also produced by other than developing countries. Actually, as illustrated in Figure 1, the LDCs can be said to control only four major

TABLE 3
Dependence on Selected Imported Industrial Raw Materials, 1975

	U.S.	European Community	Japan
	(Imports as a Percentage of Consumption)		
Aluminum (ore and metal)	84	75	100
Chromium	91	98	98
Cobalt	98	98	98
Copper	*	98	90
Iron (ore and metal)	29	55	99
Lead	11	85	73
Manganese	98	99	88
Nickel	72	100	100
Petroleum	37	93	100
Tin	84	93	97
Tungsten	55	100	100
Zinc	61	70	53

*Net exporter.
SOURCE: Council on International Economic Policy, *International Economic Report of the President*, Washington, D.C., January 1977.

commodity markets at present—again, in descending order, tin, bauxite, petroleum, and copper. Juxtaposing consumption against production, it now seems that only tin, bauxite, and petroleum—and, to a much lesser degree, copper—currently offer potential leverage to the LDCs vis-à-vis the noncommunist industrialized nations. The exact extent to which such leverage could be exercised hinges on the producing countries' export-dependence. The lesser that dependence, the greater the chances for supply manipulations. Bauxite producers now experience a rather high degree of export-dependence. With the exception of Australia, a non-LDC, all major bauxite exporters have low standards of living, no cash reserves, and heavily depend on both the revenues

FIGURE 1
LDC Share in World Trade for Selected Commodities (in Percentages)

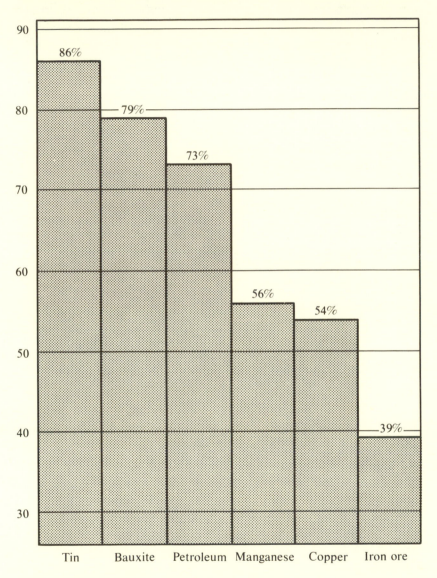

SOURCE: Adapted from Ronald J. Ridker (ed.), *Changing Resource Problems of the Fourth World*, Johns Hopkins University Press for Resources for the Future, Washington, D.C., 1976.

and the employment generated by bauxite and alumina mining and exporting: approximately two-thirds of Jamaica's, Guyana's, and Surinam's 1977 exports were bauxite and alumina. In other words, high Northern import-dependence on bauxite is matched by high Southern export-dependence, thus stabilizing trade and hindering politically induced disruption.

The same situation, although slightly better skewed to the LDCs' favor, exists with respect to tin. Six developing countries produce about 80 percent of the noncommunist world's tin. Some are heavily populated, and all are engaged in expensive development programs. Tin constitutes 54 percent of Bolivia's exports, 11 percent of Malaysia's, and 6 percent of Thailand's. This greater-than-moderate degree of Southern export-dependence somewhat reduces the potential leverage over the highly dependent North. The four main copper producers (excluding the United States and Canada) depend largely on the income from copper. They are also heavily populated, developing countries committed to costly development programs. Thus, copper constitutes 92 percent of Zambia's exports, 54 percent of Chile's, 41 percent of Zaire's, and 17 percent of Peru's.

It is only with petroleum, a commodity upon which the Northern countries are disproportionately dependent, that the LDCs enjoy a tremendous advantage due to their significantly lower degree of export-dependence. While earnings from petroleum exports still provide the bulk of the producing countries' revenues, some Arab members of OPEC have been accumulating huge cash reserves that enable them to interfere with supply over extended periods of time without damaging their own economies. This leads us to the conclusion that, insofar as the impact of the distribution of supply and demand on the present balance of resource power is concerned, only petroleum, followed by tin and, to a lesser degree, bauxite, give rise to asymmetries that could, in conjunction with the other necessary conditions, enable the South to amass sufficient resource power to confront the North.

Whether such potential will last into the 1980s or, alternatively, whether other commodities as well will present such potential by the next decade, can be determined by studying the geographic distribution of the world's mineral reserves. Table 4 gives such figures. It indicates that all four commodities discussed above will indeed remain under some degree of LDC control or influence: 79 percent of the world's reserves of tin and petroleum is located in developing countries, as are 57 percent of the bauxite and 47 percent of the copper.[14] These are the commodities that will give the South leverage against the North, provided that countries such as Saudi Arabia do not change status in the next decade. A reshuffling of the membership of these politico-economic camps will, of course, alter things. A change in the opposite direction might occur if South Africa and Rhodesia were to lose their status as developed countries and join the Southern bloc, a not so unlikely possibility under certain assumptions about political trends. Were that to happen, two additional commodities—chromium and platinum—will exhibit asymmetry between Southern exporters and Northern importers. In the case of platinum, 67 percent of the reserves of which are located in South Africa and 32 percent in the U.S.S.R., both countries have a low export-dependence, while the United States, Western Europe, and Japan are wholly dependent on imports for their domestic consumption. A more acute asymmetry is found with chromium. With South Africa controlling 63 percent of the

[14]See the IBRD statement in *Preliminary Papers*, 1st World Symposium, Energy and Raw Materials, Paris, June 1974.

TABLE 4
Distribution of World Mineral Reserves (in Percentages)

Bauxite		Other noncommunist	
Australia	30.3	countries	2.8
Guinea	22.6	Communist countries	1.3
Other noncommunist		*Cobalt*	
countries	43.3	Zaire	27.5
Communist countries	3.9	New Caledonia & Australia	27.1
		Zambia	14.0
Chromium		Other noncommunist	
Rep. of South Africa	62.9	countries	9.5
Southern Rhodesia	32.9	Communist countries	21.9

TABLE 4
Distribution of World Mineral Reserves (in Percentages) (Cont.)

Copper		Algeria	4.7
United States	22.4	Other noncommunist	
Chile	15.7	countries	28.9
Canada	8.9	Communist countries	31.2
Other noncommunist		*Nickel*	
countries	41.6	New Caledonia	33.3
Communist countries	11.4	Canada	13.6
Iron Ore		Cuba	9.1
Canada	14.5	Other noncommunist	
Brazil	10.8	countries	22.3
U.S.	3.6	Communist countries	21.6
Other noncommunist		*Petroleum**	
countries	24.5	Saudi Arabia	23.8
Communist countries	46.6	Kuwait	10.0
Lead		Iran	8.7
U.S.	38.9	U.S.	5.4
Canada	13.2	Other noncommunist	
Australia	8.3	countries	43.1
Other noncommunist		Communist countries	9.0
countries	22.2	*Tin*	
Communist countries	17.4	Thailand	33.5
Manganese		Malaysia	14.4
Gabon	15.0	Indonesia	13.2
Rep. of South Africa	8.5	Other noncommunist	
Other noncommunist		countries	21.9
countries	35.0	Communist countries	17.1
Communist countries	41.5	*Tungsten*	
Mercury		U.S.	6.4
Spain	49.1	Other noncommunist	
Yugoslavia	8.7	countries	16.1
U.S.	7.2	Communist countries	77.5
Other noncommunist		*Zinc*	
countries	21.9	Canada	26.0
Communist countries	13.2	U.S.	22.9
*Natural Gas**		Other noncommunist	
Iran	26.4	countries	35.9
U.S.	8.8	Communist countries	15.3

*Author's estimates.
SOURCE: *Morgan Guaranty Survey*, March 1974.

world's reserves and Rhodesia 33 percent, that metal shows an almost unique case of extreme geographic concentration. Rhodesia can be characterized as moderately export-dependent, chromium being one of its major exports, but South Africa is less so. The United States, Western Europe, and Japan, on the other hand, are all highly dependent on chromium imports. Thus we have another instance of an asymmetry favoring the producing countries. It should be borne in mind, however, that whether the Southern part of the African continent would ever ally itself with the LDCs is still an open question.

Essentiality

It is the third condition, that of essentiality, which is perhaps the most important in separating resources susceptible to cartelization from those conducive also to politicization. More than one commodity market may acquire the properties that facilitate the formation of a cartel, which would then apportion production and regulate prices.[15] But the extent to which the manipulation of the same commodity, through similar tactics, might extract political concessions out of consumers, and not merely commercial ones, depends not only on the economic value of that particular commodity relative to its surrogates, but also on its value compared with the political price the producers may demand. It is unlikely that any nation would alter a foreign policy based on the most fundamental national interests just because the supply of a certain commodity has been disrupted. For such an alteration to take place, indeed for economic warfare to begin at all, the commodity at stake should be one of strategic and national significance; indeed, it would be foolish to expect that interference with the supply of nonessential commodities would produce notable political benefits.

[15]The question of how many more OPECs loom in the future has sparked a very lively debate. It seems that most observers believe the prospects for cartelization in raw materials are not particularly high. A concise summary of the arguments for why cartels seem unlikely is provided by Marylin Chou, David P. Harmon, Jr., and Rudy L. Ruggles, Jr. (eds.), "Selected Resource Issues and Vulnerabilities," Hudson Institute Draft, HI-1992/4-CC, January 1975.

Essentiality indicates the relative significance of a given raw material to a nation's security and to its economic well-being. Mere application of these two criteria, however, hardly exhausts the range of politically significant raw materials. In a study conducted for the U.S. Navy, a detailed group of criteria for essentiality was submitted: an essential resource was defined as any imported raw material whose supply cutoff for a period of up to one year would have major negative impacts, whether short-term or long-term. Such effects might include serious reduction of national income or imbalance in international payments, substantial unemployment (national or sectoral), threat to military security or supply, serious and widespread political or social unrest, and major changes in the nation's economic system (e.g., the need to resort to rationing).[16] Essentiality—or criticality, a term used interchangeably—is best gauged by obtaining, as exactly as possible, measures of the damage or dislocation that could be caused by a prolonged cutoff in the supply of the resource in question. This examination requires modeling of the economy and its expected performance under varying circumstances, which obviously cannot be attempted here. Instead, reference is simply made to the list of critical materials selected, in accordance with the above criteria, by the President's Council on International Economic Policy in its *Special Report: Critical Imported Materials*,[17] a list to which resources that are commercially important were also added. Clearly, the importance of natural resources to world trade, appraised either by volume or in dollar value, always carries with it a degree of consequent political importance. The Council found 15 such critical raw materials: alumina, bauxite, chromium, platinum group metals, iron ore, nickel, manganese, titanium, cobalt, mercury, tungsten, lead, copper, tin, and zinc.

A similar and more useful inventory of essential materials was developed by Yuan-li Wu.[18] His list (see Table 5) gives the rankings of raw materials in descending order of significance

[16]U.S. Navy, "U.S. Dependence on Imported Essential Materials," mimeo. draft prepared for the Navy's Project 2000, 1975.

[17]*Special Report: Critical Imported Materials* CIEP, pp. 23–41.

[18]Yuan-li Wu, *Raw Material Supply in a Multipolar World*, National Strategy Information Center. New York, October 1973.

according to three key criteria, each one of which—scope of world production, extent of trade, and military/industrial importance—is related to the international political and economic system and comes close to meeting the standards for essentiality.

TABLE 5
Various Rankings of Minerals in World Trade

Rank	World Production By Value	By Weight	Traded Internationally By Value	By Weight	Importance in Engineering	Composite Index
1.	Iron	Iron	Iron ore	Iron ore	Iron	Iron ore
2.	Copper	Manganese	Alumina/bauxite	Bauxite	Aluminum	Copper
3.	Aluminum	Sodium	Nickel	Manganese	Copper	Lead
4.	Manganese	Aluminum	Zinc ore	Zinc	Lead	Zinc
5.	Magnesium	Chromium	Tin	Copper	Zinc	Bauxite
6.	Zinc	Copper	Manganese ore	Lead	Manganese	
7.	Mercury	Zinc	Lead ore	Nickel	Chromium	
8	Lead	Lead	Tungsten in ore	Tin	Nickel	
9.	Nickel	Potassium			Magnesium	
10.	Tin	Nickel			Tin	
11.	Potassium	Zirconium				
12.	Uranium	Lithium				
13.	Silver	Tin				
14.	Beryllium	Magnesium				
15.	Gold	Antimony				

SOURCE: Yuan-li Wu, *Raw Material Supply in a Multipolar World*.

Wu's list, it should be noted, does not refer to the subject solely from an American standpoint. Yet his composite index is not sufficient for our purposes: first, it gives only an ordinal ranking, and second, energy resources are excluded. These are corrected in Table 6.

To summarize our discussion of the essentiality of raw materials (as demonstrated by the figures in Table 6), four commodities stand out as members of a group with a higher order of criticality than the rest. These are iron ore, petroleum, copper,

TABLE 6
Priorities of Materials
(On a Scale of 1 to 10)

(1) Rank	(2) Name of Material	(3) Difficulty of Substitution	(4) Economic Importance	(5) Industrial Leverage	(6) Geometric Mean of Columns 3–5
1	Iron ore	8	10	9	8.96
2	Petroleum	8	9	8	8.32
3	Copper	6	6	7	6.32
4	Aluminum	6	6	5	5.65
5	Manganese	7	1	8	3.83
6	Nickel	4	2	4	3.17
7	Silver	8	1	4	3.17
8	Cobalt	7	1	4	3.04
9	Chromium	5	1	5	2.92
10	Platinum	8	1	3	2.88
11	Lead	5	1	4	2.71
12	Uranium	2	1	9	2.62
13	Mercury	7	1	2	2.41
14	Tin	3	1	3	2.08
15	Zinc	2	1	4	2.00

SOURCE: Adapted in part from Stanford Research Institute, *Strategic Resources and National Security*, April 1975.

51

and aluminum; of these, three are traded in large volumes by LDCs: petroleum, copper, and aluminum. The first must be considered far and above the rest in international significance. In 1975 the volume of crude oil (including liquid natural gas) produced was 2,700 million tons; of this, 56 percent—or 1,512 million tons—was traded internationally. The dollar value of such exports for that year was $125.2 billion. The comparable figures for copper are 8 million tons, with 2.4 million tons, worth $3 billion, exported; for aluminum, 13 million tons produced, 3.4 million tons, worth $2 billion, exported. Evidently petroleum is of an altogether different order of strategic significance than all the rest.

CONCLUSION

Having assessed commodities as to their physical availability, geographic distribution, and intrinsic essentiality, we are now able to compare our findings and see which commodities seem to satisfy all three necessary conditions for becoming a source of political power in a North-South context. Only one resource appears to meet all three criteria: petroleum. The other raw materials, though they may rank high on two out of three conditions, are relatively weak on the third, thereby drastically reducing their overall political usefulness. Specifically, bauxite, which comes second to petroleum in power potential, is in relatively ample supply, and so is manganese. Copper, on the other hand, is clearly both in tight supply and highly essential, but its global distribution is too diffuse to offer great political leverage.[19] And although world reserves of tin seem sufficiently restricted, and also suitably located, for deliberate LDC manipulation, tin cannot be considered to be as essential as the other commodities.

---

[19] A methodologically rigorous examination of a similar question, performed by Robert S. Pindyck, reached the conclusion that, from the point of view of gains to producers through cartelization, of the three resources examined only petroleum and bauxite offered the potential for significant monopoly profits through cartelization.

Chromium and platinum could also provide great leverage were they to fall under the control of forces antagonistic to the North; this, however, is yet to happen, and the amount of leverage they may provide is bounded by their rather moderate essentiality and scarcity. All in all, there are four resources that need to be watched—petroleum, bauxite, tin, and copper—and it is to a brief discussion of the potential problems each may present in the next decade that we turn.

In effect, none of the above minerals shows a great deal of promise as a political instrument. Even attempts merely to improve on the terms of trade through nonpolitical cartelization have so far met with modest and mixed results, and the future does not portend significant improvement in the LDCs' posture. The developing countries that export copper—Zambia, Zaire, Chile, and Peru—are organized in the Intergovernmental Council of Copper Exporting Countries (CIPEC). Together they control 30 percent of the noncommunist mine production, with a larger share—54 percent—in world copper trade. But CIPEC's control over the world's future supply is more limited—some 35 percent of the world's known reserves. The Council's objectives have been purely economic from the outset: to stabilize prices, take measures to increase earnings, and coordinate marketing and production. Yet even these limited objectives have not been achieved. The CIPEC members have failed to devise a scheme for price stabilization, and they have encountered difficulties in deciding how to share the burden of intervention; they cannot trust one another to adhere to controls and have no mechanism for enforcing agreements. The Council is simply not cohesive enough to attain goals that are clearly in the best interests of all its members. It is, therefore, even less likely to prove sufficiently cohesive on political matters, given its members' significant social, political, and ideological differences.

The situation with respect to tin is not markedly different. It is, in fact, unlikely that a cartel capable of limiting the supply of tin for political purposes will emerge. Interestingly, the outstanding feature of the world tin market, the International Tin Agreements (ITA), negotiated by both exporter and importer countries,[20] has the effect of counteracting forces that might lead to confrontation. The agreements set floor and ceiling prices; prices are controlled by buying or selling from a buffer stock. The members' objectives are to avoid price fluctuations and global or local tin shortages. At the same time, a subgroup of the producers—the three principal Asian tin producers, Malaysia, Indonesia, and Thailand—have formed a separate group, the Association of South East Asian Countries, in order to manage the tin and rubber markets for which they are principal producers. The members of the group enjoy a geographical proximity that could imply political similarity of interests. But they lack a common ideology that might have encouraged united political action.

Six countries produce about 80 percent of the noncommunist world's tin. All are developing countries committed to expensive development programs. Some are heavily populated, and all are quite dependent on tin exports as a source of foreign-currency revenues, although the three Southeast Asian countries are unevenly export-dependent: 11 percent of Malaysia's 1977 exports, 6 percent of Thailand's, and only 3 percent of Indonesia's were tin. The world's second largest producer of tin, Bolivia—obviously not a member of the Southeast Asian group—exhibits a much higher degree of export-dependence: 54 percent of its 1977 exports consisted of tin. The variance in export-dependence severely undercuts the chances for an effective, politically motivated curtailment of supply.

It is with bauxite and most notably with petroleum that we encounter a more serious potential for supply manipulation as an instrument for political coercion. As was noted above, the balance of interdependence between importers and exporters is presently lopsided, and since demand for aluminum—the end product of bauxite—is expected to grow at 6.7 percent per year, the asymmetry will probably run well into the next decade. Among Northern states, no industrialized nation—except for

[20]For a systematic analysis of the history and prospects of producers' organizations see Mikdashi's *The International Politics of Natural Resources*, particularly pp. 82–137.

France—produces more than 20 percent of its own requirements. Exports, on the other hand, are highly concentrated. Four developing countries alone (Jamaica, Guyana, Surinam, and Guinea) have over half of the world's reserves. For bauxite producers to organize a successful alliance, it is essential that Australia— a developed country—participate; only with Australia would the producing countries control a decisive portion of global reserves. It is significant indeed that Australia, under the Labour government, joined the developing countries in forming the International Bauxite Association (IBA). The IBA's declared objectives are strictly commercial, albeit quite sweeping in its demands both for higher benefits and for greater national control over the resources. It is remarkable, as one observer put it, that in subscribing to these two objectives, the Australian government has come to share the aspirations of the developing countries.[21]

It looks, then, as if bauxite offers some prospect for effective, concerted action by producers. The incentive for forming a producers' alliance is enhanced by the vertically integrated, foreign-investor-dominated nature of the aluminum industry.[22] However, the chances that such action would also assume a purely political dimension is remote since, as we noted earlier, bauxite resources are by no means scarce in relation to anticipated requirements; furthermore, it can be produced from alternative materials, and supplies can be increased significantly by intensified recycling. Without some concern over scarcity among consumers, much of the psychological, and the consequent political, leverage is lost. In addition, while Australia may indeed find it advantageous to define economic interests in common with other producers of raw materials, it is somewhat inconceivable that it would join with developing countries in demanding the establishment of a new economic order. And without Australian cooperation a bauxite producers' political association could not be a very

[21]Mikdashi, op. cit., p. 112.

[22]These, in essence, are the conclusions reached in a World Bank staff study. See "Energy and Minerals: Outlook for Developing Countries and Selected Issues," a report prepared by the IBRD's Development Policy Staff in November 1973 for the 1st World Symposium on Energy and Raw Materials, Paris, June 6–8, 1974.

effective operation. Apart from Australia, no major producer has the financial or economic strength to afford interruption of export revenues: The countries also have good working relations with private firms and are interested in more Western investment. All in all, in spite of the presence of some factors that might enable cartel action geared toward improved trading terms, there seems to be little likelihood of supply interruptions to promote strictly political interests.

We are left, then, with petroleum only. Indeed, that particular energy resource appears to be a category unto itself in presenting the potential for armed conflict resulting from the two-rung escalation process of the sort hypothesized earlier. The singularly critical political and economic significance of petroleum has been demonstrated time and again over the last few decades. It is, of course, the repeated use of oil as an instrument of political coercion by the developing Arab countries against selected developed countries of the West that underscored the disruptive effect that the manipulation of raw materials can have on international relations. More specifically, the interruption of supply revealed the potential use of oil as leverage on the policies of others. While no military reaction followed the last activation of the oil weapon, the 1973–1974 oil crisis did escalate to the point that threats to intervene militarily were voiced.[23] And yet even in such a severe application of the oil weapon no military action was undertaken.

This is not to say that oil crises in the 1980s will not trigger armed conflicts, particularly if another use of the oil weapon becomes so damaging to a consumer as to drive it over the threshold of strangulation, thereby provoking a war. This occurrence will obviously be determined by the political relations between the importing and exporting countries at that time. It is not all that clear that, by the 1980s, the leading oil-exporting nations, i.e., Saudi Arabia and Iran, will associate themselves

---

[23]For selected quotations by senior American officials on the possibility of using force as an answer to oil embargoes, see Annex A in the feasibility study on "Oil Fields as Military Objectives," prepared for the Special Subcommittee on Investigations of the House of Representatives' Committee on International Relations by the Congressional Research Service, August 21, 1975, pp. 77–82.

with the developing countries and press their grievances against the rich industrialized nations.

Assuming a different political context, whether or not the Arab oil-producing countries attempt to advance the Arab cause against Israel by using the oil weapon will hinge on the state of affairs between Arabs and Israelis at that time. It is not at all inconceivable that the conflict between them, which has been related to the previous Middle Eastern oil-supply crises, will lose some of its straining effect on regional stability in the next decade, thus reducing the motivation for resorting to acts of economic warfare against the West. Given the political need, however, to employ the oil weapon, either within a purely North-South context or as a concomitant to the Arab-Israeli conflict, the likelihood that such action will be taken will also hinge on the particular configuration of the power relationship between the oil-importing and oil-exporting countries. This, in turn, will depend on the degree of asymmetry that will characterize the conditions of their mutual dependence in the 1980s.

Interestingly, most official energy forecasts converge in projecting a worsening supply situation from about 1990 onward. But as far as the period between now and then is concerned, although the projections show an increase, in volume terms, in dependence on OPEC oil, they also show a slight decrease in the relative degree of dependence in comparison with that which prevailed on the eve of the 1973 oil embargo. The OECD expects demand for OPEC oil to increase from 30 mbd (million barrels per day) in 1976 to 35 mbd in 1985. However, by 1985, the OECD projects that its members' total energy requirements will amount to the equivalent of 5,094 million tons of oil, out of which 1,750 million tons—i.e., 35 mbd—will have to be imported. As a proportion of total energy requirements, those imports will constitute 34 percent, a drop from the 1973 proportion of 38 percent.[24] If we accept these projections, we can conclude that the 1980s will see a mild alleviation of the West's import vulnerability amid a possibly growing concern over dwindling oil reserves.

[24]The OECD's *World Energy Outlook*, published in 1977, is the most recent survey of energy projections to come from this official source.

The other side of the coin refers to the oil-exporting countries' projected export-dependence. It seems almost certain that, with the exception of the Arab countries of the Persian Gulf, all other oil exporters will experience a rather high degree of dependence on their oil resources, with all carrying large deficits. The countries that might enjoy an improvement in their state of export-dependence relative to 1970—Saudi Arabia, Kuwait, and the United Arab Emirates—may also dominate OPEC—but not necessarily control it. The reduction in these countries' export-dependence would eventually be a function of their accumulation of financial surpluses. While there have been recent speculations that such accumulation will peak by the early 1980s, with Saudi Arabia possibly experiencing deficits as that decade nears its end, it nevertheless seems more probable that these crucial nations will find an appropriate balance between their current oil income and their development expenditures without getting to the deficit point. Their future export-dependence can therefore be predicted to be as low, relatively, in the late 1980s as it was in the early 1970s, thus enabling them to engage in supply manipulations again. But the expected reduction, relative to 1973, in the importing countries' vulnerability connotes that such manipulations are likely to be less, not more, damaging than that of 1973—unless carried for a very protracted period. That is, the probability is not inevitably high that were oil to be cut off again, a strangulation situation conducive to violence would develop.

Petroleum, in sum, is indeed an exception. It is difficult to conceive of any other commodity that enables its producers to act in unison not only to improve the terms of trade but also to apply political pressure in the form of a linkage. Stephen Krasner's comment appears to be as apt for the 1980s as for the present:

Petroleum is the exception, not the rule. In other commodity markets Third World states acting alone will not be able to artificially limit supplies. Natural scarcities, corporate oligopolies, or commodity agreements between exporting and importing areas may bring higher prices, but no other group of less-developed countries (LDC's) possess the attributes that permit the oil-rich Arab sheikdoms to independently regulate the world market for a major raw material.[25]

Oil is also the exception when it comes to the likelihood that an armed conflict will result from the kind of deterioration assumed under our simple model. Precisely because petroleum can be effectively utilized as an economic weapon, it can provoke a military reprisal if it is to prove so successful as to damage consumers more than that imaginary strangulation threshold allows for. Last time around, in a rather severe application of the oil weapon, no war ensued. This is not to say that in future oil crises, with Western vulnerability not significantly lower than in 1973, no armed reaction will take place.[26] Nevertheless, it is far from certain that even repeated challenges to the oil consumers would provoke a military reaction. Other commodities, which are less suitable for waging effective economic warfare, are even less likely to precipitate a war designed to counter economic pressures.[27] The combined probability of armed encounters between North and South, then, is very low, with the possible exception of those due to oil.

[25]Stephen D. Krasner, "Oil Is the Exception," *Foreign Policy*, no. 14, Spring 1974, pp. 68–84.

[26]A balanced discussion of the future world petroleum arena is provided in Dankwart A. Rustow's "U.S.–Saudi Relations and the Oil Crises of the 1980s," *Foreign Affairs*, vol. 55, no. 3, April 1977, pp. 494–516.

[27]That is, within the South-North context. The probability that the rich countries would successfully form commodity cartels is higher than for the LDCs. Nonrenewable materials, such as uranium, and renewable resources, such as wheat, offer cartelization possibilities. Such actions on the part of the developed countries are not expected to precipitate a chain reaction leading to open war, as in the case of Third World producers. An interesting analysis of the bargaining strengths and objectives of the developing countries, which covers commodities not discussed here, is in Ernest Stern and Wouter Tims, "The Relative Bargaining Strengths of the Developing Countries," in Ronald G. Ridker (ed.), *Changing Resource Problems of the Fourth World*, Resources for the Future, Washington, D.C., February 1976, pp. 6–50.

THREE

East-West: The Scramble for the World's Resources

There is a huge map of the world, with pins in those places where "strategic materials" are located, and these are surrounded with notations that indicate the relative "strategicality" of the various materials and the relative strengths of the great powers in the areas. The new game sprang into existence when a bright young officer. . . put himself in the place of some imaginary enemy and devised a system of "Plays" whereby he could paralyze American industry. He would do this by creating circumstances in parts of the world that would deny us access to certain rare substances. . . which are essential. . . . Then he took a look at the world and found that such "Plays" were *already* being made. They were exactly what they could have been had they been guided by a single strategy bent on developing the capability to bring our whole economic system to a halt. Needless to say, the "enemy" postulated by the young game player was the U.S.S.R., and the enemy which the C.I.A.'s information shows to be behind the real-life moves is also the U.S.S.R.[28]

EAST-WEST CONFLICT AND NATURAL RESOURCES

The second current of world tension in the next decade is the relation between East and West. The competition between the

[28]Miles Copeland, *Without Cloak or Dagger*, Simon and Schuster, New York, 1974, pp. 290-291. Copeland's unique view of the world should be approached with circumspection. The anecdote quoted here, however, seems genuine and harmless to ponder over.

two major military powers could take many forms. It could also give rise to resource-related armed clashes, albeit of a completely different character than those discussed in connection with the North-South confrontation. The American-Soviet rivalry for world influence has dominated world politics for the last three decades, and it stands to reason that this multifaceted rivalry will—perhaps in different ways, and possibly on a less antagonistic level than in the past—extend into the next decade. A precise characterization of the shape this complex conflictual relationship will assume in the 1980s falls outside the scope of this discussion.[29] It is, nevertheless, fair to suppose that one of its manifestations will be a continuing effort on the part of both to expand spheres of influence, either for the sake of improving each one's own disposition or reducing the other's.

It is in such a context that natural resources and attempts to secure them might influence future superpower entanglements. In the first place, they may contribute to the conflict that already exists, thus exacerbating specific situations. Second, it is conceivable that, under some future circumstances, resources would become one of the dominant factors in superpower maneuvering in key parts of the globe, thereby generating a process resembling a scramble of sorts. Such scrambles could essentially evolve out of two fundamental predispositions: an *offensive* design, to gain control over the source of the other superpower's main imports of strategic materials in order to acquire the potential to deny the other such resources when deemed to be advantageous to do so; or a *defensive* design, to safeguard one's own sources of strategic raw materials from potential threats of denial by the other.

[29]Linda B. Miller, in her "Superpower Conflict in the 1980's" (*Journal of International Studies*, vol. 6, no. 1, Spring 1977, pp. 45–63), provides a very sensible discussion of trends in the superpower relationship. Professor Miller is quite sanguine about the direct problems that access to and supplies of raw materials will pose to the superpowers; yet she argues that "the U.S. and U.S.S.R. may not be able to insulate themselves from the conflict potentialities that will force their friends and clients" (p. 51). A most thought-provoking collection of commentaries concerning the future of East-West relations is the 100th issue of *Survey* with exactly the same title; vol. 22, no. 3/4, Summer/ Autumn, 1976.

Both modalities imply a greatly enhanced interest in particular theaters of the world, taking one or more of the many forms in which such an interest can be pursued, advanced, and—once achieved—maintained. The purpose of the following section is not necessarily to analyze the various methods that could be employed to that end, nor to identify whether the motivations behind such scrambles are offensive or defensive, but rather to identify the possible geographical loci of such conflicts and to assess their implications.

It goes without saying that for a region to be an accessible target for external penetration, it needs to lie outside already established and accepted spheres of influence, those that will hold as such for another decade. The contested areas must therefore be included in the present and future "gray areas" of the world, regions that are perceived as open for grabs. One effect of this condition rules out most, but not all, territories north of the Tropic of Cancer. At the same time, it would be absurd to regard every part of the remaining two-thirds of the globe as open to superpower maneuvering. Only such parts of the world that are currently in a sufficiently fluid state and may be expected to remain unstable for quite a while are pertinent.

While it may have appeared at one time that this fluidity was gradually receding as a function of the crystallization of post–World War II divisions, in reality the opposite has been the case. The global geopolitical scene and balance of power have actually been undergoing a drastic change, one that will probably gel only as we enter the 1980s. Delineating four basic trends in the international system—the diffusion of political, economic, and military power to the nonindustrial world; the growing importance of scarce resources; the change in patterns of Western and Soviet overseas base rights; and the rise of the new maritime regime and its impact on access to waterways, islands, and offshore resources—Geoffrey Kemp recently wrote that "although the impact of each of the trends is important, taken together the effect is dramatic. For what is emerging is nothing less than a remarkable new strategic map."[30]

[30]Geoffrey Kemp, "The New Strategic Map," *Survival*, vol. 19, no. 2, March/April 1977, pp. 50–59.

Indeed, one of the principal determinants of this new strategic map is the location of important natural resources and of the transportation routes that connect these locations with their markets. Kemp's emphasis is on the demonstrable vulnerability of the system for both sides; for the West, its oil supplies, and for the Soviet Union—its Achilles' heel, as he describes it—the external supply of food and technology. To this we might add the equally important effect that the distribution of other natural resources might have on the superpowers' interests and on the contours of the new strategic map. This leads, in turn, to a survey of the actual geographic distribution of resources in the world. Such a survey should indicate two things: first, just how dependent the great powers are on natural resources outside their territories, a dependency that might encourage a scramble for resources; and second, the location of such resources, i.e., the regions that either control the bulk of the world's deposits of a particular critical raw material or simply are endowed with an abundance of several such resources.

The outstanding feature of the way mineral resources are geographically concentrated is that five developed countries—the U.S.S.R, the United States, Canada, Australia, and South Africa—actually possess most of the world's supplies of the 25 minerals that account for more than 90 percent of the total value of all minerals consumed in the world.[31] Thus, as could have been gathered from the previous section, the world's resources, far from being at the command of the developing countries, are controlled by the great powers themselves.

The above-mentioned five countries hold more than three-quarters of the world's reserves of uranium, molybdenum, potash, chromium, and the platinum group of metals; for 12 of the 20 minerals, the five countries own more than 50 percent of total world reserves. Only in the case of petroleum, cobalt, tungsten, and tin is their share less than 20 percent of the total. Among

[31]This is M. H. Govett's major finding. For an elaboration, as well as to examine the source of the other figures used in this section, see his "The Geographic Concentration of World Mineral Supplies," *Resources Policy*, vol. 1, no. 6., December 1975, pp. 357–370.

the five, the U.S.S.R. occupies a predominant position, as illustrated by the fact that reserves of all 20 minerals occur there, with a large share of reserves for more than one-half of these minerals. The United States seems to come second with substantial deposits of uranium, lead, zinc, molybdenum, copper, silver, phosphorus, and ilmenite. Canada has significant reserves of potash, nickel, and iron ore.[32]

The reality, one that is not about to change in the next decade, is that the holders par excellence of resource power are not the developing countries but the great powers themselves. That fact, however, hardly implies that the great powers will refrain from seeking access to raw materials outside their territorial boundaries; however much they possess in natural resources, their requirements are even greater. It is that incremental demand which makes them highly interested in the resource-rich regions of the world.

In addition, the United States in particular must consider the requirements for raw materials of its allies, who are less autarkic than itself, thus significantly reducing the degree of comfort it can derive from its resource wealth. As a leader of the Western world, the United States is, therefore, keenly interested in areas that can provide the entire political and economic order it leads with vital resources. That this is so also comes as no surprise to the Soviet Union. After all, it is a tenet of traditional Marxism-Leninism that the need to obtain natural resources has been a major motive for the imperialist drives of the capitalist nations.[33] Whether the present political forms in which such needs manifest themselves are to be tolerated or opposed by the Soviet Union is a different matter. One thing seems clear: the Soviet Union certainly does not perceive itself as compelled to assist the West in politically securing its sources of vital raw materials; nor is the Soviet Union likely to fail to notice that some such areas—

[32]These figures, provided by Govett (p. 359), could be explained in part by the fact that North America and the Soviet Union have been more intensively explored than areas outside the industrial world.

[33]See Daniel S. Papp's "Marxism-Leninism and Natural Resources: The Soviet Outlook," *Resources Policy*, vol. 3, no. 2, June 1977, pp. 134–148.

as well as areas through which these resources are transported—are politically volatile at present. The West's vulnerability—exacerbated by the demise of its colonial empires and by the decline of its military power—must please Soviet defense planners.

The question, then, is exactly where these points of resource vulnerability are to appear on the emerging global strategic map. Table 7 indicates those areas south of the Tropic of Cancer where resources are concentrated. According to these figures, only three countries exhibit a preponderance of more than one critical material. They are, first and foremost, South Africa, which possesses a near monopoly over the world's chromium and platinum reserves and which has significant reserves of uranium as well; second, Australia and New Caledonia, which—though not having a monopoly over any resource—have such a rich mineral endowment, particularly in nickel, bauxite, and cobalt deposits, as to render them very inviting targets. Third in variety of resources is Brazil, which is first in the world in its iron ore resources. Then comes Zaire, rich in cobalt and copper, and Zambia, which has the same minerals but in lesser amounts. To these five one needs to add those countries that have a significant control over at least one particular resource. Several such countries stand out: Guinea (bauxite) and Rhodesia (chromium) in Africa; Saudi Arabia, Iran, and Kuwait (petroleum) in the Persian Gulf; Thailand, Malaysia, and Indonesia (tin) in Southeast Asia; and Chile (copper) in Latin America.

One cannot help noticing that all these regions are already being intensely contested by the superpowers: none of the local conflicts are devoid of direct superpower connections; consequently, the struggles are of greater intensity than would otherwise be warranted by regional considerations. In most of these the superpowers' forces are not directly involved, but rather operate clandestinely or through proxies. Furthermore, it appears very suggestive that even now the regions most intensely contested by the superpowers are those that monopolistically dominate future supplies of resources, critical to the West—specifically, the Persian Gulf and southern Africa.

THE PERSIAN GULF

The stakes in the Persian Gulf promise to be very high indeed.[34] The resources in question are obviously petroleum and natural gas, which represent enormously valuable assets monetarily and not just highly critical commodities; these resources have stirred the imagination of the leaders of the great powers since the beginning of the century, and this interest has only grown in intensity with the passage of time. Since 1973 the United States has been the more dynamic superpower operating in that theater, relentlessly pursuing the goal of drawing the key countries of the area into its orbit, establishing in the process a Teheran-Riyadh-Cairo triangle with Saudi Arabia the linchpin of its effort.

Iran has long been an ally, but even Iraq and Syria, presently pro-Soviet in their orientation, are assiduously courted by Washington. The Arab-Israeli conflict conveniently provided a vehicle through which the superpowers made friends and influenced events in the region. In the past the shipment of arms was Moscow's key instrument for acquiring clients in the area.[35] The United States has recently usurped that function and is in the process of adding the powerful instrument of arms supply to the already varied net of dependencies it has woven to advance its aims in the area, with the Persian Gulf the focus of this policy.

How the Middle East and the Arab-Israeli conflict will shape up in the 1980s is anybody's guess, but it is reasonable to assume that the center of strategic gravity will shift from the eastern Mediterranean to the Persian Gulf and that Arab-Israeli issues will deflect less attention from the Persian Gulf as local tensions build up in the Gulf area, possibly between non-Arab Iran and

[34]Middle East politics are always subject to a great deal of scholarly interest. A good summary of the issues and trends in the area is provided in volume X of the Critical Choices for Americans Series, called *The Middle East, Oil, Conflict and Hope,* Abraham Udovitch (ed.), Lexington Books, Lexington, Mass., 1976.

[35]As suggested by its title, this is the subject of Jon D. Glassman's *Arms for the Arabs: The Soviet Union and War in the Middle East,* Johns Hopkins University Press, Baltimore, 1974.

TABLE 7
Distribution of Critical Raw Materials in Countries South of the Tropic of Cancer (as a Percentage of Each Commodity's World Reserves)

	Cobalt	Iron	Lead	Zinc	Bauxite	Chromium	Platinum	Tin	Nickel	Manganese	Copper	Uranium*	Petroleum*
Central and Southern Africa													
Guinea					22.6								
Nigeria								2.1					2.8
Niger												4.8	
Zaire	27.5							3.3			5.4		
Gabon										15.0		2.4	
Zambia	14.0										7.8		
Rhodesia						33.1							
South Africa						63.1	64.1			8.5		20.6	
Persian Gulf													
Iraq													4.8
Iran													8.7
Kuwait													10.0
Saudi Arabia													23.8
United Arab Emirates													4.3

68

Southeast Asia and South Seas

Thailand						33.5					
Malaysia						14.4					
Indonesia						13.2					
Australia and New Caledonia	27.1	6.4	8.3	6.9	30.3	1.9	33.3			22.5	1.9

Central and South America

Mexico			3.5	3.1							11.0
Jamaica					6.4						
Cuba							9.1				
Venezuela											
Brazil		10.8						7.5			
Peru			2.1						6.2		
Chile									15.7		

*Author's estimates.

SOURCE: U.S. Congress, *Outlook for Prices and Supplies of Industrial Raw Materials*, U.S. Government Printing Office, Washington, D.C., 1975.

its Arab neighbors or between radical Iraq and conservative Saudi Arabia. A third potential source of tension is the growing domestic instability in the region, resulting from the rapidly building pressures generated by the hasty modernization process now under way. It is, in fact, fairly certain that the Persian Gulf area is bound to figure highly in the superpowers' considerations and bound, too, to offer ample opportunity for the competition between them to intensify.

Such an intensification, however, need not necessarily lead to an all-out, open contest, let alone an armed conflagration. Its level will most probably be affected by the nature of the local conflicts of opportunity that present themselves, with the great powers having but limited ability to manipulate these through the supply of arms or similar incentives. Moreover, one can assume that, with both the United States and the U.S.S.R. depending on the region for their oil imports, a mutual interest in limiting the potential risk of a direct, all-out confrontation would emerge, possibly inducing the superpowers to impose an upper limit on the scope of any fighting in the area. None of the great powers will find it useful to provoke or manipulate a large war in such a volatile region. It is unreasonable, therefore, to expect the great powers to deliberately induce an escalation of any local conflict. At the same time, their intensifying commitment (the United States to Saudi Arabia and, to a lesser degree, Iran; the U.S.S.R to Iraq, although relationships between Baghdad and Moscow do not even resemble the "special relationship" that exists between Washington and Riyadh), the high stakes involved—specifically, oil, the possibility of greater direct military presence, both Eastern and Western, and the probability of greater local instability—all add to the likelihood that the superpowers' rivalry will spill over into the region, thus increasing the probability of direct confrontation.

The notorious fluidity of Middle Eastern politics prevents us from predicting with any degree of precision the probable nature of the superpowers' game in the Persian Gulf in the late 1980s. That a new scramble for that region, however, is currently under way, that it could culminate in intense conflict in the next decade, and that local conditions are ripe for at least an indirect struggle over control of the region all seem reasonable propositions. Having said that, it is important to note that the tempting objectives in the Persian Gulf need not lead inexorably to a clash of interests. It has already been pointed out that, should armed conflict occur, the level of destructiveness would certainly be bounded by the superpowers' common interest in preventing damage to their future sources of oil. This cooperative ingredient may also carry over into other spheres of superpower interaction in the area, thereby further limiting the risk of an armed encounter, whether intentional or accidental. The net effect of these factors leads us to assign a rather low probability to the risk of a superpower collision over Persian Gulf oil and gas resources in the future, although this probability is greater than what now pertains.

SOUTHERN AFRICA[36]

The situation in Africa, particularly southern Africa, somewhat resembles that in the Middle East. The resources located there are in demand mainly in the West and substantially less so in the East, and the political future of many parts of the continent seems uncertain. The greater number of states offers a wider range of operation. The political fluidity of southern Africa and its multitude of resources may mean that the scramble to establish connections there could be more frantic and—potentially—more aggressive than similar activities in the Persian Gulf.

An appreciation of the present importance of southern Africa can be gained by observing its share of global production of several minerals in 1976. The region accounted for 62.5 percent of the world's total production of natural diamonds, 60.8 percent of the gold, 50 percent of the vanadium, 45.7 percent of the platinum-group metals, 36.2 percent of the chromite, 35.3 percent of the cobalt, 24.4 percent of the manganese, 18 percent of the

[36]Throughout this discussion the term southern Africa is meant to include the following states: Angola, Botswana, the Congo, Lesotho, Mozambique, Rhodesia, South Africa, South West Africa (Namibia), Swaziland, Tanzania, Zaire, and Zambia.

71

copper, 13.7 percent of the uranium oxide, 5.8 percent of the nickel, 4.5 percent of the zinc, and 1.6 percent of the lead.[37]

The most lucrative future objective within that area is South Africa, which is not only the dominant producer of gold, vanadium, platinum, chromite, and manganese in the region, but is also—insofar as future supplies are concerned—in a near-monopoly position with respect to chromium and, to a lesser extent, platinum. South Africa controls upwards of two-thirds of the world's reserves of chromium as well as some two-thirds of the world's platinum reserves. Thus, the United States could eventually become totally dependent on the willingness of the South African government to furnish these minerals. Furthermore, as indicated in Table 7, South Africa also happens to command one-fifth of the world's uranium resources. The fact that South Africa also dominates the oil routes going around the Cape, thus indirectly controlling the global distribution of oil as well, enhances its geostrategic significance even more.

It is a plain fact that the region is in turmoil; local instability will probably last well into the 1980s. It is also evident that the superpowers have been very active in the area and that they are probably cognizant of the significance of the region's raw materials. The inviability of the present regime in Rhodesia over the long term and probable trouble in South Africa offer ripe conditions for an almost direct superpower competition to secure allies and establish the necessary footholds in the region. The Soviet Union enjoys a tactical advantage in not being tied to the burdensome white-minority regimes as the United States has been. Recently, however, Washington revised its policy and took a long-term view of its interests by favoring majority rule—thus leading the United States into a middle-term period of tense relations with the white regimes—in the expectation that the shift in policy will restrict the U.S.S.R.'s maneuvering room, and possibly pay off in the future, when majority rule is established.

[37]Data quoted in "The Mineral Connection," *The Economist,* July 9, 1977, p. 83, relying on the following sources: *Mining Journal Annual Review;* U.S. Bureau of Mines—*Commodity Data Summaries; World Metal Statistics.*

While it may be hard to sort out the resource considerations from the other issues involved in southern Africa, the level of attention given to that part of the world by the superpowers and the deliberate and often subtle way each uses the instruments of influence at its disposal—under the constraints that limit either of them—suggest that the game is for stakes much higher, and for objectives more mundane, than the establishment of representative democracy.

AUSTRALIA AND THE INDIAN OCEAN

Table 7 suggests yet a third area of such immense resource wealth and of such geopolitical importance as to bring it into growing international attention—Australia. Commanding an impressive array of critical materials, it accounts for 65 percent of the noncommunist world's reserves of rutile titanium, 36 percent of the bauxite, 30 percent of the uranium, and 16 percent of the iron ore. It also has deposits of copper, nickel, and alumina, and the prospects for the discovery of oil and natural gas are also promising.[38] The geopolitical attributes that make Australia appear to be a gray zone are twofold: first, it is situated in a theater in which direct United States involvement has declined and Soviet influence increased; second, and related to the first, with a population of less than 14 million inhabitants, Australia is a militarily weak country. Though an ally of the United States (through the ANZUS Treaty), Australia must have had its doubts over the value of that alliance ever since President Nixon proclaimed the Guam Doctrine. At the same time, Australia has been watching with apprehension the growth of the Soviet presence in the Indian Ocean, at one point regarding it as directly threatening to her

[38]The data are provided in "Australia Survey," *The Economist,* March 27, 1976, p. 4, and quoted in the International Economic Studies Institute (IESI)'s *Raw Materials and Foreign Policy,* Washington, D.C., 1976, p. 119. See also the discussion of Australia's policies as a major resource supplier, pp. 118–127.

and calling for an increased American presence to counterbalance the Russians.

So far, American thinking has been revolving around the idea of a joint Soviet-American reduction of naval forces in the Indian Ocean. Whether the Soviet Union will respond favorably is still an open question. For the time being, a quiet competition between the great powers to establish bases and to sway allies around the Indian Ocean is noticeable. While at present this contest is centered at the Western littoral of the ocean, around the Horn of Africa, a similar development occurring at the eastern littoral is not implausible. Australia, itself long-engaged in a reexamination of her own predispositions, would be placed in a very awkward position were the Soviets to gain the upper hand in the Indian Ocean and its periphery. The risk that Australia's security would, indeed, be compromised under such circumstances could alert the United States—and, possibly, Japan too—to the possible effects on the supply and price of resources, thereby adversely sparking increased superpower activity in the Indian Ocean.

Common to all three key, critical, resource-rich regions thus far identified is that they border on the Indian Ocean. Indeed, with the Persian Gulf to the north, South Africa to the west, and Australia to the east, the Indian Ocean now appears to be the most important body of water on the strategic map. The fact that the strategic oil and commercial sea-lanes leading to Japan, Western Europe, and North America crisscross that ocean further augments its significance.

Deployment of substantial naval forces into the Indian Ocean is a possibility, prevented from occurring so far mainly by considerations of geographical feasibility or convenience. It is not so much the key points on the littoral of the ocean which attract superpower presence, but rather the ocean itself. Such a presence, at least as far as the United States is concerned, becomes even more attractive when the option of deploying strategic forces, such as SSBNs (nuclear-propelled ballistic-missile-bearing submarines), in the ocean—thereby complicating Soviet defense problems—is contemplated. If the United States and the Soviet Union forego effective disengagement agreements concerning their naval forces, the Indian Ocean is likely to become the focus of increased superpower competition for its control. This competition may take a riskier form if attempts are made not only to control the high seas but also to establish bases and military facilities along the littoral states or on the many islands and islets previously held by the colonial empires. These areas are increasingly significant due to their potentially strategic location and the advantages that may accrue to their control in connection with new legislation from the UN Conference on the Law of the Sea to extend national territorial privileges further into the sea.

The Indian Ocean, much as it may become the core of the new strategic map, is not self-contained. The proximate parts of the South Atlantic and the South Pacific are of similar potential significance because they comprise the access waterways to the Indian Ocean and because they, too, are dotted with territories that have only recently gained independence. The potential strategic importance of these territories often outweighs their value as independent entities politically as well as economically. As such, these territories, although peripheral to the Indian Ocean, possess great importance in and of themselves; over the long run, as will be argued below, they may prove to be the most contentious territories remaining.

For resource-related conflicts to develop within an East-West context—so it has been argued thus far—it is necessary that the resources be located in areas whose legal and political status is in flux; this, after all, is the essence of the new gray areas to be contended for by the superpowers, albeit in an indirect and restrained manner. In addition to the triangle of resource-rich littoral regions encircling the Indian Ocean, two other gray areas par excellence—both known to contain rich mineral deposits—are likely to emerge as potential theaters of superpower contention: Antarctica and the seabeds.

ANTARCTICA

Antarctica is bound to attract heightened international interest for two reasons: first, its legal status is the subject of conflicting territorial claims (with the United States and the Soviet Union both enmeshed); second, the possibility exists that a variety of resources will be found there. Whether this interest will assume conflictual rather than cooperative attributes by the 1980s depends on several factors, most important of which are the superpowers' perceptions of the adequacy of their resource base and the state of relations between them. If by the 1980s the present concern about resource scarcity becomes greater, and if superpower relations grow even more competitive, then it is not folly to predict a scramble for Antarctica's riches.

One reason that the late 1980s might see greater tension over Antarctica is the existence of a deadline that, like other political deadlines, may precipitate a conflict that might otherwise have been postponed. The deadline is 1991. The Antarctic Treaty freezes, in effect, all territorial claims to that continent until then. The number and force of such claims are certain to grow as that deadline approaches. It is, however, not clear that the United States and the Soviet Union will necessarily find themselves on opposing sides.

At present, the economic interest exhibited and political pressures exerted by various nations focus on the resources of the Antarctic sea—e.g., the possibility of harvesting krill—rather than those of the land.[39] But interest in the exploitation of land-based resources is also growing, since the continent may contain hydrocarbons and other minerals. The Russians are reported to have found a "mountain" of iron ore in one area, and indications are that it exists in others. Although no exploration for oil has yet taken place, all signs point to the existence of vast offshore fields. Traces of other valuable minerals have been found.[40] Yet little is known of the extent of such resources, and difficult working conditions combined with political restrictions make it infeasible to exploit them in the near future.

In 1959, twelve countries signed the Antarctic Treaty in Lon-

[39]The krill is of immense potential significance. A tiny, shrimplike crustacean, it is exceptionally rich in protein. The potential annual catch of Antarctic krill has been estimated at between 50 million and 100 million tons—without dangerously depleting the stock; the total existing world catch of fish and shellfish in 1974 was only slightly more than 60 million tons.

[40]Marcel Berlins, "Antarctic Cooperation Threatened," *The London Times*, March 21, 1977.

don: Britain, France, Belgium, Norway, Australia, New Zealand, South Africa, Argentina, Chile, Japan, the Soviet Union, and the United States. Poland is a new Consultative Party to the Treaty. The Treaty was designed to preserve the Antarctic for peaceful scientific work. It also provides not only for keeping the areas free of nuclear weapons but also for mutual inspection of scientific installations. But it contains no rules about commercial exploitation. The Treaty has worked well because the Treaty powers were left to themselves and because, until recently, only a few nations were interested in what went on in Antarctica. However, it is already becoming evident that the signatory states are about to respond to the growing pressure of outside interests and possibly also to their own needs. Still, the exploitation of Antarctica's resources presents several difficulties: first, the determination of what the resources of the Antarctic may be and of what effects exploration and exploitation may have on the environment; second, and more serious, seven of the signatories—Australia, Argentina, Chile, France, New Zealand, Norway, and Britain—have made territorial claims that are not recognized by the other Treaty members (specifically the United States, the Soviet Union, Japan, South Africa, and Belgium). The Treaty froze these territorial claims until 1991, but they could very well surface earlier, bringing about a rift between nonclaimant powers and the rest of the signatory members as well as between the signatory members and others in the international community who see Antarctica as part of the human heritage in the same sense that the seabed is regarded.

The Ninth Antarctic Treaty Consultative Meeting, held in London in October and November of 1977, imposed restraints on mineral exploration and exploitation in the area until environmental impact studies are carried out. This decision implies that the covert divisions among the signatories will be kept so until the early 1980s. This is only an interim measure and a temporizing device, for it leaves the central question of resource allotment untackled.[41] In the future, pressures are only likely to accumulate, and it remains to be seen whether a group of nations

[41]As reported by Paul Cheeseright in the *Financial Times* (London), October 10 and 11, 1977.

77

so diverse as the signatory members to the Treaty will agree on a regime that will regulate the exploitation of Antarctica's sea and land resources and that will, at the same time, be internationally recognized. Failure to reach such an agreement could signal that a scramble for Antarctica's resources is imminent. While this scramble may not get under way by the next decade, the extent of its inevitability may be clearer by then. Once this clarification happens, and given the expectation of a scramble, its occurrence could be accelerated in the familiar manner in which future expectations are sometimes "telescoped" in terms of time, i.e., by becoming realities sooner than expected.

Interestingly, however, so long as that scramble is contained, continuing disputes over territorial claims in Antarctica will not pit the United States against the Soviet Union; instead, they may cooperate in opposing the claimant group of seven. Thus, although Antarctica clearly comes as close as possible to our definition of a gray area, disputes over it will not be conducted along neatly divided East-West lines. Rather, the bargaining groups that are likely to emerge will cut across ideological, political, and military alliances, which may attenuate the intensity of the risk of escalation inherent in such situations. The net effect of all this is that Antarctica may well become a battleground of conflicting territorial claims, but the likelihood that such disputes will involve the threat of use of military force would be small indeed.

THE SEA

If it is the undefined nature of sovereignty rights which makes Antarctica a most likely place of contention, the other such gray area, where the problems of sovereignty and the privileges that ensue therefrom are even more acute, is the seabeds. Again, among the bargaining and caucusing groups that have coalesced around this issue, the United States and the Soviet Union are to be found in the same camp. This alone is enough to reduce significantly the danger of war otherwise associated with disputes over such high stakes. Indeed, the earth's seas are known to contain at least 30 common minerals—in the seawater itself, as sediments on the ocean floor, within bedrock, or under the ocean floor. From the standpoint of immediate international concern it is the presence of offshore resources that is most likely to cause political friction. Chief among the offshore resources is petroleum. The exploitation of resources on the deep seabed, most important of which are the so-called manganese nodules, will probably create international difficulties only in the long term. The more serious difficulties, however, are likely to arise by the 1980s, most probably in connection with "coastal" disputes, especially over the exploitation of offshore petroleum. In 1973, offshore production accounted for 18 percent of total world production. That percentage is on the rise and is expected to increase considerably, perhaps as high as 50 percent, in the next decade.[42]

Most problems with the orderly exploitation of offshore resources stem from the inadequacy of the criteria for determining the extent of continental-shelf resource jurisdiction. The frantic search for indigenous oil resources on the part of most industrialized nations now extends into the sea, and as the competition for new petroleum sources accelerates, so, too, does the potential for conflict, particularly among states with adjacent or facing continental shelves.[43] As long as there is no new, universally accepted and implemented treaty on the Law of the Sea, the issue of exploitation and exploration of oceanic resources, whether offshore or in the deep sea, will remain fraught with conflict. Disputes about the exploitation of oceanic resources have already occurred: between the Federal Republic of Germany, Denmark, and the Netherlands concerning shelf boundaries in the 1960s; and between Greece and Turkey, Libya and Tunisia, and Britain and France—to name a few—in the 1970s. The number of such disputes will certainly increase severalfold by the 1980s. It is not inconceivable that any of them may de-

[42]IESI, *Raw Materials and Foreign Policy*, which quotes the National Petroleum Council's *Ocean Petroleum Resources*, Government Printing Office, Washington, D.C., March 1975.

[43]For more material on the legal issues invoved in the Law of the Sea, see John Temple Swing's "Who Will Own the Oceans?" *Foreign Affairs*, vol. 54, no. 3, April 1976, pp. 527–546.

teriorate into local armed confrontation; it is impossible, however, to predict which particular dispute will trigger a war, because, more often than not, the disputed resources will serve only as a catalyst for a conflict whose background is to be found elsewhere. Important as these materials may be, it is not easy to imagine that neighboring countries will risk a war just for offshore resources.

Ironically, the potential for conflict over resources will not necessarily disappear with the creation of a satisfactory treaty on the Law of the Sea. While such legislation may ultimately put an end to the ambiguities and inconsistencies now present, the possibility of establishing a 200-mile economic zone could induce coastal states and others capable of doing so into a rapid scramble to secure and claim sovereignty over barren islands and islets in order to greatly enhance their offshore privileges. In fact, the prospects for such a scramble are high irrespective of progress made on the Law of the Sea. The treaty would probably influence the tempo of that scramble; the sooner it is agreed upon, the more intense it will be. Indications that such regional races may already be under way can easily be observed by counting the increasing number of conflicting sovereignty claims involving islands that have hitherto been considered *nullius res*.

That most of these disputes are inherently local is clear. Consider, for instance, the Red Sea. The hot brine pools discovered on its floor contain a mixture of metal compounds, principally oxides and sulfides of iron, manganese, zinc, and copper. The value of these sediments, estimated for one location only, has been placed at $2.5 billion worth of zinc, copper, lead, silver, and gold at 1972 prices. Red Sea politics, however, are confined to the countries along its shores. The great powers have not shown any particular interest in its geothermal resources, and whatever interest they have in the constellation of power in the Red Sea relates more to the pivotal Horn of Africa, the strategic importance of which is considered to be of *global* significance; the Red Sea, its resources, and the politics relating to it, on the other hand, are treated as *regional* in scope.

There are actually only two or three areas where the Soviet Union faces either the United States or other major Western nations. One such area is the Arctic region: both the United States and the U.S.S.R. flank the Polar Sea. In that strategic region, where economic and military interests are intertwined, Spitzbergen's continental shelf and the Barents Sea are already being disputed, and Norway's decision to explore for oil north of the 62nd parallel has already elicited Soviet saber rattling, indicating that the Soviet Union, at least, is not shy about threatening the use of force to protect what it perceives to be its resource interests. If, however, future military activities there cannot be ruled out,[44] this is primarily because of the region's strategic importance—it is a spot where the NATO countries meet the Warsaw Pact countries—and not because of its petroleum or fishing resources.

The Japanese claim to the Kurile Islands, held by the Soviet Union since the end of World War II, is, perhaps, the most notable instance of a territorial dispute directly involving the Soviet Union with a Western country. But neither the Kuriles nor Japan is the real focus of the coming struggle for the as yet untapped and unclaimed resource-rich territories on the globe. Rather, it is the entire Pacific basin that is increasingly becoming the likeliest candidate for Soviet penetration in the foreseeable future. So long as Japan stays essentially unarmed and the People's Republic of China remains a purely continental power, there remains only one power capable of expanding its influence in what has been, until recently, an "American Lake"—the Soviet Union. The buildup of the Soviet Pacific naval capability is sufficient evidence that it is doing precisely that.

The benefits accruing to the power more successful in establishing its influence over the Pacific Ocean and the numerous Pacific islands exposed to such expansion of influence may not be immediately visible; they are, nevertheless, potentially enormous, particularly in the long run. Again, it would be an artificial analytical exercise to separate the resources and their value from

[44]Martin Ince, "Why the Barents Sea Has Suddenly Become a Hot Spot," *The London Times*, December 19. 1977; also Kemp, op. cit., p. 58. This thesis is forcefully argued by Ulrich Schweinfurth in his "New Pacific States and the Super Powers," *Aussenpolitik*, vol. 28, no. 2, 1977, pp. 203–214.

other strategic considerations. Nonetheless, as far as the quest for resources in the Pacific is concerned, the issue appears in two geopolitical modalities: The first pertains to the jurisdictional claims and disputes over the continental shelf and the chief resource found there—oil. Exploitation of offshore oil and gas is already technologically possible and economically viable, hence the relatively greater urgency on the part of claimant countries either to assert their claims or to urge appropriate legislation at the UN Conference on the Law of the Sea. Such disputes in the Pacific, however, are, by their very nature, likely to be local— i.e., not involving the great powers—the Spratley Islands being a possible exception.[45]

The second, and more likely, superpower competition may be for the resources of the seabed. Unlike utilizing offshore resources, mining on the seabed is far from being a near-term proposition; consequently, the political pressures to secure those parts of the seabed where resources may be found are considerably less powerful than for the continental shelf. Seabed mining is at present viewed as "a technological infant, an economic question mark, and a jurisdictional no-man's land."[46] Yet it is this last attribute which may ignite a scramble for the high seas even before the advent of economic profitability and technological feasibility.

Among the yet untapped seabed resources, those that hold the greatest promise in economic terms are the ferro-manganese nodules. These nodules are known to contain four minerals in

[45]The old dispute between the People's Republic of China (PRC), Vietnam, and the Philippines over the Spratley Islands is showing signs of reviving in the wake of indications that the area may contain oil deposits to the tune of 7 billion barrels. Consequently, the Philippines government was reported to have already occupied six islands in the Spratley group and to have built up strong forces on Palawan, partly to protect its offshore oil fields and partly to keep an eye on the Spratleys (David Houseg in the *Financial Times*, September 6, 1977). The PRC, which claims all islands in the South China Sea, has so far asserted her authority only by occupying the Paracels in defiance of a Vietnamese claim. Expectedly, Taiwan has also put in a bid for the Spratleys. Less typical, but more indicative of the trend, is the British interest in the rock island Rockall in the North Atlantic.

[46]IESI, op. cit., p. 243.

commercially attractive proportions: manganese, nickel, copper, and cobalt. A typical deposit of commercial interest contains 25 to 30 percent manganese, 1.0 to 1.5 percent nickel, 0.5 to 1.0 percent copper, and 0.25 percent cobalt.

The most likely locations for early commercial mining of seabed resources are in the Pacific Basin. In an area that extends from Baja, California, to the Hawaiian Islands and beyond, and from the equator to 20 degrees north, there is a heavy concentration of manganese-nodule sites at depths between 12,500 and 17,500 feet. This area covers some 12 million square kilometers.

Other areas containing rich deposits are believed to exist in the South Pacific and probably in the Indian Ocean. The extent of those resources, while not precisely known, is clearly enormous, with some minerals—e.g., nickel—existing in quantities exceeding those found on land.[47]

While the hypothetical production levels from nodules, illustrated in Table 8, may be large indeed, recent studies indicate that the number of projects that will come into operation in the late 1980s will be small although they will be on a relatively large scale.[48] It is the combined effect of the actual beginning of commercial exploitation and the magnitude of potentially recoverable resources which could galvanize political interest in these areas within a decade.

Nevertheless, intensifying international agitation over the Pacific Basin seas and the exploitation of their resources will—as in the case of Antarctica—probably not give rise to situations conducive to war in the time frame discussed here. Political maneuvering around the Indian Ocean, a region which itself is growing

[47]Ocean Mining Administration—Department of the Interior, *Manganese Nodule Resources and Mine Site Availability*, August 1976, and Congressional Research Service, *Ocean Manganese Nodules* (2d ed.), February 1976, cited by Michael Hardy in his "The Implications for Alternative Solutions for Regulating the Exploitation of Seabed Minerals," *International Organization*, vol. 31, no. 2, Spring 1977, p. 315.

[48]Hardy, op. cit., p. 316. Interestingly, thus far the pressure for project development comes more from private enterprises, such as Lockheed, than from governments. For Lockheed's plans, see Peter Hill's "Digging Around for Riches in the Ocean Deeps," *The London Times*, May 26, 1977.

TABLE 8
Hypothetical Mineral Production from Nodules (in Metric Tons)

	Nickel	Manganese	Cobalt	Copper
Potential Production Starting in 1980				
Minimum authorization (share of world market)	42,000 (4.6%)	320,000 (2.5%)	5,500 (12.5%)	36,000 (0.3%)
Maximum authorization (share of world market)	84,000 (9.2%)	640,000 (5.0%)	11,000 (25.0%)	72,000 (0.6%)
Potential Production by 1985				
Minimum authorization (share of world market)	175,000 (14.3%)	1,300,000 (7.9%)	23,000 (33.0%)	150,000 (1.0%)
Maximum authorization (share of world market)	350,000 (28.6%)	2,600,000 (15.8%)	46,000 (66.0%)	360,000 (2.0%)

SOURCE: UN Secretariat, *Economic Implications of Sea-Bed Mineral Development in the International Area*, A/Conf.62/25, May 22, 1974.

in geostrategic prominence—is currently focused on the Horn of Africa, with both the United States and the U.S.S.R. manipulating their regional allies as they jockey for positions of improved command over that body of water. The deliberations of UNCLOS do not even take the form of a competitive American-Soviet confrontation. Rather they appear more as a North-South issue, with the developing countries, particularly those that are large exporters of resources, concerned that large-scale seabed mining might lead to losses in their revenues by exerting a downward pressure on prices.

Still, the problem of establishing a legal regime for the deep seabed, which lies beyond the 200-mile economic zone, is not solely a North-South problem. A race can be expected to develop along East-West lines, particularly in the Pacific, with increasing naval defense problems probable as commercial seabed mining is begun, but possibly sooner. The Pacific is ripe for such a race. Many of the new nations in the Pacific cannot, under any circumstances, be considered politically and economically viable. This precarious existence may tempt the superpowers into practicing aggressive power politics. The trend of events thus far has consisted of gradual American disengagement from Southeast Asia and creeping Soviet entry into the Pacific. Sooner or later, however, as Soviet penetration begins to endanger Western economic and military interests, the United States withdrawal may stop; a struggle for control of the Pacific may very well take place. The jockeying for position that is now occurring will gain in momentum, with a corresponding increase in the risk of confrontation and war. That process, as one Western analyst noted, seems like an extension of the final distribution of land masses into the ocean areas:

The search for and securing of raw materials resources will promote still further this distribution of ocean areas, including every inch of the seabed. In connection with such efforts every atoll and every little rock only just awash gains enormous importance, especially in conjunction with hugely expanded territorial limits. This results in tremendous interest in Pacific islands and archipelagos, be they large or small, until they have been fully apportioned in one way or another, as independent entities or otherwise.[49]

[49]Schweinfurth, op. cit., p. 211.

FOUR

South-South: Regional Powers and Natural Resources

Yet another situation where, *prima facie,* force might be used to gain access to resources involves the emerging regional powers. It is possible that states with a clear military advantage in a given region will resort to the use of military might in order to secure resources located within their sphere of influence. It is also possible that neighboring states will engage in violent disputes over resource-rich territory. Our concern here is specifically with the future course of action of regional powers. However, since the potential exercise of armed might by newly emergent powers represents a possibly critical discontinuity—or new dimension—in the international system of the 1980s and beyond, this kind of armed conflict over resources appears more probable than those hypothesized in the context of North-South and East-West relationships. The East-West contingencies are constrained by the nuclear balance and the upper bounds it puts on the likelihood of direct military clashes. North-South contingencies are also constrained by the South's economic—not to mention military—weakness, which limits the effectiveness of whatever resource power it has. It is hard to think of any use by the South of whatever resource power it has which will provoke military retaliation by the North. These constraints seem to be absent in the hypothetical case of a country that enjoys some sort of regional predominance and entertains hegemonic ambitions. It can presumably utilize to the fullest its regional advantage and intervene to gain access to resources.

To be precise, an additional qualification is in order. For a regional hegemonic power to demonstrate a propensity to intervene so as to get access to resources, two conditions need to be met: that certain resources are required by that power and that those requirements could be satisfied by intervening where it is inclined to. This, in turn, means that autarkic or nonindustrial hegemonic powers would feel less pressure to intervene for the sake of obtaining resources. In other words, the paradigmatic case of a hypothetical hegemonic power that might intervene for such purposes would be the import-dependent, highly industrialized military power whose raw material imports originated in a country within its sphere of influence.

Once this is understood, it immediately becomes clear that this category is, in reality, almost an empty set. No single country among those expected to display hegemonic tendencies in the next decade can fit that characterization. While in principle there is nothing implausible in such a characterization, it is a matter of geopolitical reality that political and military predominance usually go hand in hand with natural-resource predominance. This phenomenon was noted earlier when it was stated that the United States and the Soviet Union are the two leading countries with respect to indigenous natural resources. But the phenomenon also extends to regional powers such as Brazil, Iran, and Indonesia. Four other countries may be potential hegemonic powers—Japan, India, Australia, the People's Republic of China—yet they do not seem to be exemplars of the category as defined above; each is in a different situation, and all are unlikely to be prone to such hegemonic intervention.[50]

---

[50]Ray S. Cline, in his *World Power Assessment: A Calculus of Strategic Drift* (Georgetown University, The Center for Strategic and International Studies, Washington D.C., 1975) attempted to measure the international power of nations as the aggregate or product of six component elements—perceived power, population and territory, economic capability, military capability, strategic purpose, and the will to pursue national strategy (pp. 7–12). In his final assessment, countries outside NATO and the Warsaw Pact that emerged as comparatively powerful were the PRC, Brazil, Iran, Japan, Australia, India, and Indonesia. It seems safe to assume that these countries will endure in their capacity as potential hegemonic powers in the 1980s.

The PRC is largely autarkic in its resource needs, which are themselves quite modest because of its less than fully industrialized economy. Aside from its efforts to ensure its oil-exploitation rights in the South China Sea, a policy that cannot be termed strictly interventionist, it has no sufficiently great need for resources from the outside world, it does not exhibit obvious hegemonic ambitions beyond its immediate border, and there are no resource-rich countries in the vicinity to whet Chinese appetites.

India is a somewhat different case, closer to our original notion of an import-dependent country with a tried and proven military potential. Except for iron, aluminum, and manganese, of which it has substantial deposits, India has to import most of its raw materials. It is particularly lacking in oil, copper, zinc, lead, tin, and nickel. In short, it presents a clear picture of serious resource deficiency, and although parts of the country—particularly the Himalayan regions—remain unexplored, the prospects for improvement in India's deficiency are slim. India has asserted its power in the subcontinent, but its feud with Pakistan and that country's own potential checked, to some extent, its aspirations. It is India's misfortune that much as it may possess hegemonic aspirations, the country is encircled by powerful neighbors, some with similar ideas of their own—Pakistan and Iran to the west, the People's Republic of China to the north, and no real outlet to the south. But if there is one major reason that precludes serious consideration of the possibility that India will embark on an interventionist venture to secure resources, it is that the need for them is not too acutely felt. India is still a developing country; furthermore, the potential objectives of interest—i.e., those with the resources that might attract its attention—Iran and Indonesia—are both militarily powerful and potentially capable of putting up so much resistance as to make the costs of intervention too high relative to the expected benefits.

The second class of potential hegemonic powers—Indonesia, Iran, Brazil, and Australia—includes no country readily identifiable as one with the will and the wherewithal to engage in resource interventions. The reason is simplicity itself—all four countries are exceedingly rich in resources and none suffers from acute import-dependence on raw materials. These countries feel no apparent need to capitalize on their regional military advantage to obtain resources; in fact, in large measure, their status as regional powers is at least partly due to their comfortable resource position. The assumed line of causality between resources and hegemony, in fact, shows a reversal in their case.

Indonesia is the fifth most populated country in the world. It has a large army. Its mineral wealth is vast; yet, at the same time, agriculture is still the backbone of the nation's economy, which is at subsistence level. The last two factors negate whatever interventionistic impetus the first two may have implied. Though less than 10 percent of the land area has been explored to date, significant deposits of tin, copper, bauxite, nickel, gold, silver, uranium, granite, coal, manganese, and—most important—petroleum and natural gas have already been discovered.[51] Indonesia's oil reserves are put at 12 billion barrels and her natural gas reserves at 0.6 trillion cubic meters. With daily production of more than 1.5 million barrels at present and with double that rate projected for the late 1980s, oil is the resource that, if high prices hold, will provide Indonesia with the capital necessary to develop its other resources. Tin is Indonesia's second most important raw material. With 13 percent of world output, it is the third largest producer of tin in the world. The country could expand its tin production to 320,000 tons per year within a year or two, but it abides by export controls imposed by the ITC. The 1.2 million tons of bauxite it produces annually represents 2 percent of world production, a proportion that is not going to change in the next decade. Nickel mining, on the other hand, is an expanding industry, and so are copper and coal mining.

All in all, Indonesia's vast potential will be fully exploited if prices remain at reasonable levels and if it can surmount the problem of locating the large sums of capital investment necessary for such development. The country's long-term future as one of the world's major mineral producers is not yet assured, but it certainly has that potential. The political ramification of

[51]Bruce Lloyd, "Indonesia's Mineral Resources," *Resources Policy*, December 1975, pp. 326–342.

these bright prospects is that Indonesia feels no need to exert force outside its borders for the purpose of procuring natural resources. At most, it would take an activist view of the political implications of expanded territorial limits on the continental shelf, but such an attitude is to be expected from any but the most supine coastal states, not just from hegemonic powers.

The case of Iran is different only in degree. It is rich in natural resources other than oil. Its known gas reserves (17 trillion cubic meters) are second in the world only to those in the U.S.S.R.; and over the next decade, Iran will emerge as a leading world supplier of gas. Other minerals already found include copper, whose deposits are estimated at 400 million tons; iron ore (but the bulk of the country's needs are imported); coal, to the point of near self-sufficiency; lead; and gold.[52] Iran's principal resource and the mainstay of its national economic power is oil. With proved and probable reserves estimated at 63 billion barrels, Iran ranks third in the world.

It is paradoxical, therefore, that a move to grab its neighbor's oil fields—Iraq's or Saudi Arabia's—is believed by some to be the probable manifestation of any hegemonic designs harbored by Iran. The rationale offered for this action is that Iran's grandiose military and economic development plans may entail expenditures that will exceed the country's oil revenues, thus forcing Iran to seek other sources of income. Such a rationale, which is the only one ascribing to Iran designs to capture natural resources belonging to others, cannot be viewed as other than purely speculative and dubious, for Iraq is already a formidable military opponent, and Saudi Arabia is acquiring a pretty effective defensive capability of its own. It is not that Iran has no hegemonic ambitions; rather, it is that these ambitions are channeled into policies aimed at safeguarding its interests as a resource supplier, not an importer. Accordingly, its strategic attention has focused on the Persian Gulf and the littoral countries dominating the oil sea-lanes.

One seasoned observer noted that Iranian intervention in the

---

[52] A most useful set of facts, figures, and observations about Iran are provided by the Hudson Institute's survey, "Iran," compiled by Andrew Caranfil et al., HI-2107/2-CC, March 5, 1975.

affairs of the Persian Gulf and the Indian Ocean is to grow apace with the expansion of Iranian military and naval power.[53] That may be the case, but military operations have so far been confined to the Persian Gulf theater, and a move against India or Afghanistan is a very remote possibility. At any rate, such moves would not be motivated by a quest for resources. Iran's role as a hegemonic power with abundant resources, in sum, will not result in *offensive* military interventions to gain access to resources belonging to others. If any military intervention is to occur, it will be for the purpose of assuring access by others to its own resources.

As with Indonesia and Iran, natural resources constitute the vehicle that can catapult Brazil to world-power status. Enormous in size (3.3 million square miles) and with a large population base (109 million), Brazil has the "critical mass" to become a global power; but unlike India, which possesses the same two properties, Brazil is potentially rich in a wide variety of minerals, and that makes a big difference. Having had a spectacular growth rate for the last 10 years or so, Brazil seems to have reached the takeoff point in its economic development. Were it deficient in raw materials, this progress might have connoted interventionist pressures to secure badly needed resources; but the fact of the matter is that Brazil's future resource requirements could and are likely to be met indigenously. At present, the bulk of Brazil's mineral endowment remains underdeveloped, and Brazil is a net importer of most minerals: It is import-dependent for 68 percent of its copper, 35 percent of its lead, 100 percent of its metallic nickel, 77 percent of its zinc, and so on. This import-dependency, particularly on oil, represents a substantial drain on Brazil's foreign-exchange earnings.[54] But the country's vast mineral wealth is yet to be exploited. Full mapping surveys have been carried out over only a limited area; the Brazilians, therefore, unlike the Iranians, are unaware of the full extent of their country's wealth. Brazil has untapped deposits of bauxite, tin,

[53]Dana Adams Schmidt, "Iran, Self-Appointed Guardian of the Gulf," *Christian Science Monitor*, January 29, 1975.
[54]IESI, op. cit., pp. 138–147.

zinc, iron ore, and nickel, as well as oil, and it seems to be firmly set on the path that will make it one of the world's major suppliers of raw materials by the end of the century.[55]

Brazil's estimated proven and probable petroleum reserves are generally assumed to be not larger than 1 billion barrels; the corresponding estimate for natural gas reserves is 0.2 trillion cubic meters.[56] But Brazil has 1.4 million square miles of sedimentary basin, much of it unexplored, as well as a promising continental shelf. It is expected to increase production to more than 500,000 barrels daily by the early 1980s, thus meeting almost half of its consumption. Brazil's strength lies in other raw materials. It is already the largest exporter of iron ore in the world; it exported $837 million worth in 1977, and it expects to be exporting $5 billion worth by the mid-1980s. Manganese has traditionally been its second largest mineral export, and Brazil is the third largest producer in the world after the Soviet Union and South Africa. Exports have averaged about 1 million tons annually, and this level should be maintained in the future, as the country's total manganese reserves are estimated at 180 million tons.

Brazil also has one of the largest reserves of the best-quality bauxite in the world. Furthermore, it has all the basic inputs needed for the production of metallic aluminum at a competitive price for the world market, and the trend of rising levels of imports is expected to reverse itself soon. Brazil also has large reserves of nickel ore, amounting to approximately 300 million tons, containing about 4.5 million tons of metallic nickel; it may also have sufficient chromium reserves to become a major producer. It appears that almost irrespective of world trends over the next decade, Brazil will be undertaking a substantial expansion of its mineral sector. A large proportion of this production—for most minerals—will be processed and consumed locally.

[55] A detailed review of Brazil's natural resource endowment and the present government's policy with regard to the exploitation of minerals is given in "Brazil's Mineral Development: Potential and Problems," by Bruce Lloyd and Erica Wheeler, *Resources Policy,* March 1977, pp. 39–59.

[56] This is a very conservative estimate. Lloyd and Wheeler argue that reserves in the Campos Basin alone amount to 3.5 billion barrels; p. 49.

However, analysts point out that, in the 1980s, an increasing range of minerals will become available for export, and Brazil could have a considerable impact on the nature, direction, and prevailing patterns of international trade in minerals.[57]

Brazil is also a regional hegemonic power, and its influence is on the rise. The military is compact in relation to Brazil's size and population, and in marked contrast to Iran, Brazil's defense spending is no more than 2 percent of gross domestic product (GDP). Apparently this is enough, for the Brazilian armed forces are the most powerful in Latin America, capable of coping with Bolivia, Paraguay, Peru, Colombia, and Venezuela in the unlikely event that Brazil is required to fight on all these remote frontiers at the same time.[58] Brazilians are cognizant of their growing economic and political power and adapt themselves ideologically to such prospects. But there are no signs whatsoever that such hegemonic aspirations will take the form of defensive resource-related military activities, let alone offensive operations.

Compared with other countries in their vicinity, neither Japan nor Australia can field too impressive an army. Their status as potential hegemonic powers stems not so much from their military prowess as from their advanced, modern industrial base, their economic strength, and other ingredients of power: for Japan, population; for Australia, territory. Yet when it comes to resource availability, they are at opposite ends of the spectrum. Australia, as noted earlier, has abundant natural resources and ranks third or fourth in the world in the versatility of endowment of natural resources. It is an exporter both of renewable resources, such as wheat, and of nonrenewable resources; furthermore, Australia does not have an expansionist, hegemonic legacy, nor is it likely to acquire such tendencies in the next decade.

Japan, on the other hand, is lacking in raw materials and is acutely sensitive to that predicament; it bears a recent legacy of expansionism—one embarked upon with the explicit aim of securing the raw materials in which it was deficient. Japan, in fact,

[57]Lloyd and Wheeler, op. cit., p. 59.
[58]This is David White's assessment, expressed in the *Financial Times* survey, "Brazil," November 8, 1977.

is the only power that might have a motivation strong enough to move aggressively in order to obtain the raw materials needed to maintain its economic viability; it does not, however, have the capability to do so.

In broad outline, while Japan's raw-material requirements are substantial, it has virtually no indigenous industrial raw materials. It is this combination of great demand for resources and exceedingly high degree of import-dependence which renders Japan's a uniquely vulnerable economy. This is illustrated by the fact that it is the world's second largest market, after Europe, for raw materials: more than half of Japan's imports are of raw materials. The United States and Western Europe import 15 and 75 percent, respectively, of their raw materials.[59] And as was noted earlier, Japan is more than 90 percent import-dependent in bauxite, chromium, cobalt, copper, iron, nickel, tin, tungsten, and, of course, petroleum. It also has to import heavily other minerals—lead, 73 percent of requirements; manganese, 88 percent; zinc, 53 percent.[60]

This extreme degree of dependence has imbued Japan with a sense of defenselessness (sometimes termed *happo yabure*). Its own past efforts to secure raw-material sources through imperialism failed with its defeat in World War II. At present Japan is engaged in resource diplomacy, whereby a combination of diplomatic measures and financial and economic instrumentalities is utilized to advance its interests and reduce as much as possible the adverse security and foreign-exchange effects of high import-dependency. This diplomacy is sometimes pursued aggressively, as incidents with Indonesia, Australia, and Brazil attest. Japan hopes that the politics of economic security, particularly vis-à-vis Australia, will adequately achieve what the politics of imperial aggrandizement failed to do.[61]

[59]IESI, op. cit., pp. 178–179.

[60]These figures are from the *International Economic Report of the President* and refer to 1975, p. 187. MITI, however, provided even starker numbers: 79 percent for lead and 69 percent for zinc. See IESI, op. cit., p. 180.

[61]In addition to practicing traditional diplomacy, Japan is manipulating its investment and contract policies to provide greater resource security. It con-

It is not a mere preference among optional instrumentalities. Japan is no longer the hegemonic power it was 35 to 40 years ago. The continental countries of Asia have grown militarily stronger while Japan has semivoluntarily disarmed. Its high dependence on imported raw materials is not going to change; neither—or so it seems—will its low defense profile, which effectively renders it incapable of military intervention to gain access to the sources of raw materials, certainly not on the scale attempted a generation ago.

Were Japan to rearm, the military option would reappear, but it would still remain doubtful whether the balance of power could allow successful Japanese hegemonic interventions.[62] In all probability, the Japan of the 1980s will remain aware of its extreme vulnerability—and lack the necessary regional military muscle to do much about it.

The prospects for hegemonic interventions to gain access to resources seem, in conclusion, slim indeed. Potential hegemonies such as Iran, Indonesia, Brazil, the People's Republic of China,

---

tracts on a long-term basis, and it carefully selects the candidates for resource investment. Thus, Canada and Brazil are the most attractive countries for those Japanese firms involved in resources. A survey by *Nikkei Business* ranked 53 major countries on seven measures (political situation, economy, resource availability, etc.). The results largely confirm what many observers thought, that Brazil is preferred to Australia. In its relations with Australia, Tokyo is capitalizing on the fact that Australia is as much in need of Japan's markets as Japan is of resources and that Japan may have alternative sources whereas Australia does not necessarily have alternative markets. In the aggressive pursuit of such manipulations vis-à-vis those countries that depend on Japan more than Japan depends on them (the Philippines, New Caledonia, and—in part—Australia), Japan has met with some consternation among the export-dependent producer countries, but these resource-procurement tactics are the manifestations of economic hegemony and come to compensate for the absence of a military hegemony. See the *Financial Times* survey, "Japanese International Companies," December 21, 1977.

[62]Herman Kahn's *The Emerging Japanese Superstate* (Prentice-Hall, Inc., Englewood Cliffs, N.J., 1970) raises and analyzes Japanese defense problems and the possible "elevation" of the defense posture (see pp. 160–180).

and India have the military potential but not the sufficient need to apply it for that purpose, and those with the need—Japan, for example—lack the military potential. None of the basic conditions is likely to change in the near future. This cannot be said about the long term, particularly in reference to Japan's capabilities.

FIVE

Conclusion: Preventing Armed Conflict over Resources

It has already been noted that many observers consider the resource problem more dangerous and urgent than can be learned from this essay. Indeed, neo-Malthusians carry their prophecies to apocalyptic lengths, seeing salvation from catastrophe in rather radical schemes.[63] Their sense of crisis stems from the premise that human beings, through their exponential growth, are overtaxing the world's limited "life-supporting" resources. There is another camp—already identified—that demands revolutionary actions: the group of developing countries that perceives a global-equity crisis for which the resource issue could be both an opportunity and an instrument for change. Resolution of the resource crisis would, by itself, eliminate the otherwise high danger of conflict it entails, or so contend members of this group.

At the other end of the spectrum one finds observers who do not consider the issue to be so critical as to justify a radical reordering of the world's institutions or the alteration of lifestyles. To them, the strains currently being experienced—and those that can be expected—in the resource area are symptomatic

[63]See, for instance, the premise and proposals put forth in the second report of the Club of Rome, *Mankind at the Turning Point*, by Mihajlo Mesarovic and Eduard Pestel (E. P. Dutton & Co., New York, 1974). Also far-reaching in its suggestions is the so-called RIO Report (standing for "Reviewing the International Order"), Interim Report, prepared during the second general meeting held in Rotterdam, June 17–20, 1975.

of the transition from the industrial era to the postindustrial era and have more to do with the relative lag in response on the policy level of existing institutions to the process of change than with resources per se.[64] For these analysts the crisis in resources is merely a failure of policy and practice, nothing else. Their solution, therefore, is managerial; they provide suggestions for corrective measures ranging from institutional innovations to more practical adaptive steps. Here, too, the danger of armed conflict, already significantly lower than that felt by the former group, is assumed to be further reduceable by improvements in the state of affairs at the managerial level, not the structural or the distributional level. Both approaches are aimed at reform, but the former group's approach is inherently revolutionary whereas the latter group's is inherently conservative.

The paradox of the revolutionary platforms is that, in attempting to alleviate a global crisis that is perceived in apocalyptic terms, proponents of such reforms call for drastic actions that might themselves lead to war; at the very least, the massive systemic restructuring they seek would create upheavals conducive to violence. Would it not be ironic if it turned out that the premises underlying both revolutionary platforms—the one stressing ecological equilibrium and the other stressing economic equity—turned out to be false? That is, if it were shown that the system is no more significantly "overloaded" today than it was, say, a millennium ago—which seems to be the case—or that the LDCs' challenge to the developed world goes beyond a simple desire to have a more equitable distribution of wealth. It would seem then that revolutionary reform, which, ipso facto, includes the creation of conflict-producing situations, could endanger peace almost as much as its absence.

The other reformist movement, as noted above, is quite conservative in orientation compared with the revolutionary school; the remedial actions advocated by such analysts (e.g., the enlargement of stockpiles, the drive toward autarky, etc.) are aimed

[64]Typical among these is Herman Kahn, as illustrated in his monograph "A World Turning Point—and a Better Prospect for the Future," with W. Brown, Hudson Institute HI.2185/2-P, January 1975.

100

at the prevention of overreaction of the kind likely to be precipitated by those who accept neo-Malthusian premises. For it is such overreaction that could endanger the smooth and presumably efficient operation of the commodities market and threaten investments in production; moreover, Third World producers could capitalize on the neo-Malthusian thesis to aggravate the market structure by legitimizing political oligopolies instead of seeking to secure economic competition and the depoliticization of trade, as consumer countries would like. Some of these remedial actions go even further and include defensive measures— often referred to as "resource diplomacy" or the politics of economic security—to protect consumers from the alleged wrath and baleful influence of raw-material producers. In addition, there are numerous suggestions to confront the challenging cartels through the institutionalization of a system of collective economic security.[65]

Common to all nonrevolutionary schemes is the belief that no new order, "economic" or "international," is needed. The institutional bases for action already exist. An essentially conservative approach, therefore, is recommended not necessarily because of one's attachment to atavistic predispositions but, by and large, because of the realization that no threat of natural shortages exists, that the phenomenon of cartelization is not necessarily the "wave of the future," much less the remedy to its problems, and that present institutions—including the state system—could adequately contain the disruptive risk inherent in transient dependence on industrial raw materials.

It is, therefore, not so much the malaise of the West that accounts for the passivity with which it reacted to the LDCs' challenge as the belief that the challenge is not as menacing as others have put it; first, because raw materials do not offer an

---

[65]Writing in *Foreign Affairs* (April 1974), Richard N. Gardner noted that "where countries are found to have violated the new principles and fail to adjust their policies in accordance with multilateral decisions, they should face the possibility of multilateral reprisals." See his "The Hard Road to World Order," p. 566. J. S. Nye went even further in defining the nature of such multilateral action in his "Collective Economic Security," *International Affairs*, October 1974, pp. 584–598.

omnipotent lever; second, because the developed countries still maintain most of the economic trump cards, not to mention the military ones. Ultimately, the purpose of conservative reformists is to defuse whatever threat of supply manipulation exists, since they regard it as the main threat to peace, as opposed to the revolutionary reformists, who see in these very manipulations a way to achieve global harmony and tranquillity, having forgotten that the crisis in petroleum was precipitated primarily by the cartelization of the world market through OPEC.

Petroleum will remain the most sensitive and, thus, the most potentially destabilizing commodity in the future: there will be no reduction in its powerful political utility. The probability of a strangulation scenario—a *casus belli* by definition—in the late 1980s cannot be completely minimized, although it is quite possible that the cartel will lose some of its grip on the market and that importers will succeed in diminishing their vulnerability, either through greater autarky and reduced import-dependence or through such defensive means as stockpiling, diversification of sources, and multilateral emergency sharing programs. If oil is to act as a catalyst for future armed conflicts, their locus, obviously, would be the Middle East. No other raw material is likely to trigger a war between the developed and the developing countries.

An East-West scramble for resources and for the resource-rich regions of the world could, in and of itself, increase friction between either the superpowers themselves or their regional allies. The arena for this competitive bid for control over resources would be the several critical areas on the "new strategic map" whose tenuous political status or attractive mineral deposits make them enticing as targets of such a scramble: the Persian Gulf, South Africa, Australia and the Indian Ocean, Antarctica, the Southern Seas, and the Pacific Islands. If the scramble proceeds at its present pace, then no major war involving the superpowers is likely to occur. However, the fact is that the currently slow tempo of the scramble—proxy wars in Africa, clandestine operations in Southeast Asia and Latin America—is due to the lack of a sense of urgency in the struggle for the world's resources, the cautious approach of the superpowers' leaders, and the atmosphere of détente that formalizes these. There is no guarantee that these will last into the 1980s; actually it may be predicted with some confidence that the sense of urgency will increase and that Soviet caution might recede as new leaders come to power in Moscow and the naval buildup provides the U.S.S.R. with greater capabilities. It is quite likely, therefore, that an intensification of the scramble and the frictions it engenders will characterize the next decade.

One can hypothesize basically two ways to limit an East-West conflict over resources and contain its risks. The first involves incorporation of the matter into the set of issues toward which the superpowers have adopted a predominantly cooperative attitude and, through formal accommodation, seek to restrain the scramble or at least to mitigate its adverse consequences. A variety of possibilities present themselves, ranging from international legislation, such as the Law of the Sea, to regulate the orderly exploitation of resources in hitherto undefined areas to the resolution of those local conflicts that permeate the pivotal geostrategic points. The second approach presupposes that it would be impractical to assume superpower cooperation and not an ongoing competition. In such a circumstance, which seems more realistic, the main hope for the maintenance of stability—in spite of a continuing scramble—is for a rough balance of power to prevail, either in mutual capabilities and military deployment or in the resource leverages gained by the superpowers and in the degree of resource vulnerability experienced by them. The pursuit of such a balance could itself spur the scramble, but so long as it is achieved and maintained, a resource strangulation scheme on the part of one great power against the other will appear counterproductive, leaving the only risk of armed conflict on the local level. If it happens that one of the powers achieves superiority through the scramble for resources, then resources will assume an inordinately critical strategic significance, not in precipitating a nonnuclear or limited war but in determining its scope, shape, and possibly its results if it breaks out for other reasons.

South-South conflicts resulting from the attempt by hegemonic powers to gain access to and control over resources are also quite unlikely. Such attempts may not be beyond the already manifest hegemonic aspirations of some countries—e.g., Brazil and Iran—but it just so happens that those countries with the most potential for becoming hegemonies are extraordinarily rich in natural resources; if they are to engage in interventionistic ventures it would clearly not be for the sake of obtaining resources. Japan may be an exception, but it does not invalidate the rule: though it is acutely deficient in resources and critically dependent on them, it is not militarily paramount in the region, and the force of arms is no longer—if it has ever been—a feasible option for it.

The undeniably growing importance of raw materials and the politics of using or securing them will probably be conducive to a less stable world as tensions increase both on the regional and on the global level. There will be more international disputes involving access to resources. But all are likely to fall short of causing major upheavals that may lead to war. The historically modest role natural resources play as the direct occasions for war is not about to become larger, at least not for another decade. In the North-South confrontation, it is not that resources are marginal to the conflict, but that they are simply insufficiently powerful to raise the confrontation to the level of military operations—petroleum being the only possible exception. The East-West confrontation has always had a military aspect, albeit for other reasons, and resource considerations are unlikely to have a major impact on the confrontation, although they may shift the theater of operations southward. The more intense the superpower rivalry becomes, the more intense the scramble for resources. That intensity, however, will be predominantly determined by factors other than resources. Lastly, no hegemonic military interventions to exploit resources are in the cards, not even from Japan, the only country for whom resources may be vitally critical and which has shown a predilection for such interventions in the recent past.

Alternative Commodity Trade Regimes

Rachel McCulloch and José Piñera

ONE

Introduction

Although formal and informal attempts to control markets for individual primary commodities have been an important feature of the international economy throughout the century, there is now strong pressure in the world community to use commodity trade as a whole as a vehicle for meeting the economic and political demands of the developing nations. At the same time, the unprecedented market disruptions of recent years have given rise to considerable interest on the part of industrialized nations in measures to ensure adequate supplies of essential raw-material imports at stable or at least predictable prices.

The current drive to institute new international rules governing commodity trade reflects two basic characteristics of primary commodities. First, commodities constitute the only broad class of internationally traded goods supplied in disproportionate amounts by less developed countries (LDCs). These nations together account for less than 20 percent of world trade but supply more than 40 percent of total world exports of primary commodities. With members of the Organization of Oil Exporting Countries (OPEC) excluded, the proportions are similar: non-OPEC LDCs account for less than 12 percent of total world trade, but almost 20 percent of world exports of primary com-

NOTE: This paper was prepared for the 1980s Project of the Council on Foreign Relations. Tables are from Rachel McCulloch, "Commodity Power and the International Community," in N. Kamrany (ed.), *The New Economics of the Less Developed Countries*, Westview, Boulder, Colo., 1978.

modities. Furthermore, despite considerable success by a number of developing nations in promoting exports of manufactured goods, primary commodities still generate about 60 percent of the total export earnings of non-OPEC LDCs.[1] A shift in the terms on which commodities are traded thus holds the potential for effecting a significant redistribution of world income from the industrialized to the developing nations.

The second reason for special attention is that primary commodities as a group are typified by sluggish responses to price on the part of both consumers and producers, especially over short time periods. This economic characteristic, technically termed *inelastic demand and supply*, underlies the sharp price fluctuations common to most primary commodity markets. These price fluctuations furnish an important motive for attempts at market control.[2] Both producers, who suffer from corresponding fluctuations in export earnings, and consumers, who face unpredictable variations in the prices of required imports, see real benefits to be gained from increased market stability. Furthermore, inelastic demand and supply provide conditions highly favorable to successful manipulation of market forces, particularly actions intended to raise price and thus increase gains to suppliers at the expense of consumers.

In recent years, the developing nations have sought to link the commodity issue to other economic and noneconomic objectives of the LDCs. Failure to develop new trading arrangements satisfactory to all interested parties may therefore have deeper consequences for future economic and political relations between the industrialized and developing nations. If dissatisfied commodity exporters threaten or adopt such unilateral strategies as supply interruptions, embargoes, or discrimination among consuming nations to improve their bargaining power in other areas,

[1]Table 1 shows LDC exports of "primary commodities in the broad sense" as defined by the United Nations Conference on Trade and Development (UNCTAD), SITC 0-4. In fact, this definition understates somewhat the importance of LDC primary exports, since it excludes exports of slightly processed metals, SITC 68.

[2]As Table 2 indicates (see p. 120), many LDCs depend upon exports of a single primary commodity for the bulk of total foreign-exchange earnings.

importing nations may attempt to exercise their own economic leverage in food exports, market access, or financial flows. Escalation to political or even military retaliation could also result. Such action might then trigger further LDC responses, including collective default or massive expropriations. While a scenario of escalation remains conjectural, the possibility, however remote, of provoking an all-out confrontation provides another motive for current international efforts to reach some compromise on commodity trade.

Because both developing and industrialized nations as groups now perceive that significant advantages can be gained from new international rules governing trade in primary commodities, it is likely that important policy choices will be made in this area during the next decade. The purpose of this paper is to assess the desirability of alternative international arrangements in terms of the underlying objectives of collective action. In Chapter 2 we examine four distinct and, to some extent, conflicting objectives that have been prominent in the international negotiations on primary commodity trade: international income redistribution, stability for exporting nations, security for importing nations, and overall economic efficiency. Chapter 3 explores the structure of alternative commodity trading "regimes." Four regimes are identified according to the degree of control exercised by interested parties: the competitive market, unilateral producer control, unilateral consumer control, and negotiated control. We describe measures used individually or in combination to control market outcomes and evaluate the alternative regimes in light of the four objectives. In Chapter 4 the components of a "preferred" regime are outlined.

TABLE 1
LDC Exports of Primary Commodities, 1973 (in Millions of U.S. Dollars)

Commodity Class	Exports from	Exports to				
		World	Developed Market Economies	EEC	USA	Japan
Total trade *(SITC 0-9)*	*World*	572,650	408,560	204,580	69,960	34,460
	All LDCs	108,790	81,430	34,560	21,520	14,960
	Africa	20,360	16,650	11,390	2,190	1,030
	America	29,060	22,130	6,810	10,970	1,570
	Middle East	27,030	20,180	10,690	1,270	5,060
	Other Asian	31,300	21,540	5,380	6,960	7,020
	OPEC	42,650	34,300	16,650	6,570	6,870
Food, beverages, and tobacco *(SITC 0-1)*	*World*	76,960	54,570	31,670	8,680	5,570
	All LDCs	20,640	14,980	6,950	4,380	1,660
Cereals *(SITC 041-045)*	*World*	15,670	7,060	4,070	36	1,870
	All LDCs	1,750	760	485	4	140
Crude materials except fuels; oils and fats *(SITC 2 + 4)*	*World*	57,950	44,340	22,280	5,200	10,010
	All LDCs	17,720	11,950	5,270	1,700	3,480
Oilseeds, nuts, and kernels *(SITC 22)*	*World*	4,900	4,120	2,330	71	1,110
	All LDCs	1,170	1,000	680	63	145

Textile fibers (SITC 26)	World	11,470	7,590	3,880	240	2,060
	All LDCs	3,200	1,790	910	64	500
Crude fertilizers and minerals (SITC 27)	World	4,160	2,940	1,600	420	335
	All LDCs	1,370	820	350	185	140
Metalliferous ores and metal scrap (SITC 28)	World	11,220	9,340	3,920	1,290	3,070
	All LDCs	3,710	3,250	1,100	610	1,220
Animal and vegetable oils and fats (SITC 4)	World	3,740	2,630	1,820	245	155
	All LDCs	1,330	1,030	690	185	39
Mineral fuels and related materials (SITC 3)	World	63,100	50,320	23,460	10,660	8,100
	All LDCs	43,040	34,800	15,580	7,890	6,790
	OPEC	37,820	31,240	15,310	5,780	6,180
Primary commodities (SITC 0-4)	World	198,010	149,230	77,410	24,540	23,680
	All LDCs	80,800	61,730	27,800	13,970	11,930

SOURCE: UN Statistical Office, *Monthly Bulletin of Statistics*, July 1975.

TWO

Objectives of Collective Action

International debate on the establishment of new commodity trade arrangements has centered on four distinct objectives in terms of which any proposed action must be judged. These objectives are international income redistribution, stability for exporting nations, security for importing nations, and overall economic efficiency.[3] Of the four objectives, redistribution appears to be the major concern of the developing nations, who also emphasize stability of foreign-exchange earnings for commodity exporters. The industrialized nations also see redistribution and stability as desirable goals. The motives range from humanitarian to strategic; however, it is security in their role as primary commodity importers that provides the central motive for participation in current negotiations. Gains from increased efficiency would accrue to both consumer and producer nations; unlike redistribution, gains in efficiency result in a larger "economic pie" to be divided among the world's nations. In practice certain industrialized nations stress efficiency aspects for rhetorical purpose, but there is little evidence that economic efficiency is a primary concern of policy makers in either group.

[3]A similar analytical framework is presented in Carlos F. Díaz-Alejandro, "North-South Relations: The Economic Component," *International Organization*, vol. 29, Winter 1975, pp. 213–241.

REDISTRIBUTION

The primary thrust of the drive to establish a "New International Economic Order" is to reduce the existing disparity between the affluence and power of the industrialized nations of the "North" and the less developed nations collectively termed the "South."[4] The achievement of this goal depends both on international redistribution of the income generated by existing wealth and on internal economic transformation of poorer nations to enhance their own ability to create new wealth. In the area of primary-commodity trade, the main objective for the South is an increased share of the income generated by existing wealth, to be achieved through higher prices for commodity exports. However, the possibility also exists for primary commodities to play a role in internal transformation through increased processing of raw materials in the countries that produce them.

It is perhaps worth noting explicitly that the desirability of redistribution from richer to poorer nations, whether through higher commodity prices or any other transfer channel, does not rest upon such considerations as whether the terms of trade of commodity-exporting nations inevitably worsen over time, as argued by Prebisch and his followers,[5] or whether present markets are best described as competitive, monopolistic, or monopsonistic. However, the current distribution of income has been determined in part by these factors. Also, the perceived inequity of present arrangements may reflect the belief that existing market imperfections favor the North at the expense of the South.

Much discussion has been devoted to the relative merits of higher commodity prices as a vehicle for effecting a desired redistribution. It has been widely recognized that the North-

[4] In this paper we use "South" to refer to the bloc of less developed nations. These nations are still also known collectively as the "Group of 77," although member nations currently number well over 100. "North" here refers primarily to the industrialized market economies that make up the Organization for Economic Cooperation and Development (OECD).

[5] For a discussion of the Prebisch position, see Harry G. Johnson, *Economic Policies toward Less Developed Countries*, The Brookings Institution, Washington, D.C., 1967.

South aggregation of redistribututive consequences masks important arbitrary and even regressive elements in the outcome. Despite the disproportionate reliance of developing nations on primary exports, the industrialized countries still produce by far the larger *absolute* share of these products. The largest absolute share of the transfer generated by higher commodity prices would go to a few developed nations—Canada, Australia, South Africa, and perhaps the Soviet Union—rather than to nations of the South. Costs to be borne by consuming nations will reflect their degree of dependence upon primary commodity imports, rather than national wealth or "ability to pay." The poorest LDCs, many of which rely upon imported oil, food, and industrial raw materials, would be made poorer still by a general policy of higher commodity prices unless accorded preferential treatment. There is a precedent for such special treatment in the various policies implemented after 1974 to aid oil-importing LDCs.

In terms of internal redistribution, the impact of higher commodity prices could well be regressive. Within countries of the North, higher prices for nonfuel primary commodities would have a larger relative impact on lower-income groups than on more affluent consumers. Likewise, there is no assurance that the benefits gained by exporting nations would necessarily flow to the poorest groups within those nations rather than to powerful economic and political elites. The precise incidence of higher commodity prices depends crucially upon the way higher prices are achieved and the methods by which consuming nations adjust. In general, the outcome will reflect the degree of commitment, both within nations and in the international community as a whole, to the goal of income redistribution. Differences in the redistributive impact of alternative measures to raise commodity prices are discussed in Chapter 3.

In light of the ambiguous redistributive consequences of higher commodity prices, other measures to induce international redistribution would appear preferable. However, the alternative channels may be at least as unsatisfactory. Indeed, interest in commodity trade as a potential channel for redistribution between North and South has been heightened by the almost universal perception that alternative measures have become increasingly difficult to employ. In the past, emphasis has been placed on direct aid flows and "soft" loans at below-market interest rates to augment the foreign-exchange earnings of poor nations and on expansion of "nontraditional" exports of manufactured goods by developing nations to the industrialized world.[6] Today the prospect of increases in direct aid flows or soft loans appears dim. Northern nations are greatly disillusioned with these measures, in terms either of humanitarian achievements or of strategic and economic benefits to themselves; likewise, many developing countries now see bilateral flows of this type as undesirable because they are invariably accompanied by restrictions and obligations that reduce their economic value and undermine the sovereignty of the recipient.

The prospects for rapid expansion of manufactured exports from LDCs to the industrialized nations are at best uncertain. Within the United Nations Conference on Trade and Development (UNCTAD), the developing nations have promoted the Generalized System of Preferences (GSP), a plan that allows their manufactured exports to enter the markets of the industrialized countries duty-free or at reduced tariff rates. After more than a decade of delay, all the major developed regions have implemented some type of GSP scheme. However, restrictions on eligibility of countries and commodities have greatly reduced potential gains from the GSP. Particularly important is the exclusion from eligibility of a number of import-sensitive items that have already caused severe internal adjustment problems for the industrialized nations. In effect, precisely those labor-intensive manufactures in which the LDCs have already achieved considerable market penetration even in the absence of preferences— i.e., those in which they have the greatest demonstrated comparative advantage—are explicitly excluded from preferential treatment. Thus, the established routes for industrialization have

[6]It should be noted that expansion of manufactured exports is, in itself, not a channel for North-South redistribution. However, preferential market access may entail an "aid" component. See Rachel McCulloch and Jose Piñera, "Trade as Aid: The Political Economy of Tariff Preferences for Developing Countries," *American Economic Review*, vol. 67, December 1977, pp. 959–967.

been increasingly blocked. For the LDCs themselves, accelerated industrial development may also be seen as requiring costly internal adjustments. Changes in established economic and social relationships can undermine political stability. Hence, both Northern and Southern policy makers may see in higher commodity prices a transfer channel that entails a smaller degree of internal dislocation than rapid export-oriented industrial development by the South.

EFFICIENCY

An obvious goal for any economic arrangement governing trade in primary commodities is to promote economically appropriate production and consumption patterns. One important and much discussed aspect of economic efficiency is an appropriate time profile of production, that is, avoidance of too rapid depletion of natural resources as well as of overly conservative policies that result in underproduction of needed raw materials. Private or national producers will determine the intertemporal pattern of production according to the rate of discount that they apply to future profits. Whether current production is too high or too low relative to true social needs depends upon whether the discount rate applied by producers to future profits is greater or less than the appropriate social discount rate needed to compute the present value of future benefits.

For any given level of total production, productive efficiency requires that the total "social cost"—the sacrifices of other output, including both marketable goods and such unmarketed goods as clean air and water—be minimized. To achieve cost minimization, production must be allocated internationally in such a way that, at the margin, social cost is the same in each producing area. In practice, this requirement is unlikely to be satisfied under existing arrangements or any foreseeable alternatives. For efficiency in consumption, each user must pay the true social cost of commodities purchased. Again, this condition is unlikely to be fulfilled under any foreseeable commodity regime.

Many discussions of alternative arrangements center on the

efficiency implications of commodity-price fluctuations. Although unanticipated price changes pose serious problems for producers and consumers alike, price fluctuations also contribute to economic efficiency. By providing information concerning relative scarcity or abundance, price changes initiate appropriate modifications in the behavior of producers and consumers. For storable commodities, price fluctuations induce private inventory accumulation or disposal to reallocate available supplies of commodities to periods of highest economic value. International action to depress fluctuations of price around a long-term trend thus implies some sacrifice of valuable market information and induced responses in return for greater ease in planning by producers and consumers. A further complication is that international efforts to stabilize prices can have the opposite effect, so that the costs of intervention are incurred without the possible benefit of more predictable outcome. This is particularly likely when stabilization authorities are slow to recognize a long-term change in conditions.

Ironically, the perceived need for multilateral stabilization agreements results in part from the activities of government agencies, rather than from the market. Because some type of government intervention is probable whenever prices are unusually high or low, private stabilization activity tends to be depressed below the level that would be justified by its social rate of return. While it would perhaps be preferable to limit the power of governments to engage in erratic regulatory activities in the first place, compensatory action in the form of stabilization agreements may reduce the damage.

STABILITY

Markets for primary commodities are characterized by inelastic demand and supply—that is, amounts bought and sold are relatively unresponsive to price changes, at least over short periods. Therefore even minor disturbances in demand or supply conditions can require relatively large price movements to "clear the market." For most commodities, the business cycle in the industrialized nations is the major factor determining fluctuations of world demand around its long-term trend. Weather is the most important source of short-term supply disturbances for agricultural products, while political upheavals may affect supply of both agricultural and mineral raw materials.

A major concern raised by instability in commodity trade is the impact on foreign-exchange earnings of developing nations. The literature of economic development and the rhetoric of recent international negotiations have underscored the disproportionate dependence of LDCs on export earnings generated by primary commodities. As Table 2 indicates, individual developing countries often depend on exports of just one or two commodities for a large fraction of total foreign-exchange earnings, making that total highly vulnerable to short-term fluctuations in export prices. The implications of this vulnerability depend upon the opportunities for reserve accumulation or external borrowing as means of smoothing fluctuations in export earnings around a trend. However, most Southern nations experience perennial balance-of-payments deficits and thus find it difficult or impossible to accumulate holdings of international reserves as a means of coping with earnings fluctuations. Likewise, most LDCs cannot afford to rely heavily on short-term borrowing in international capital markets to cover export-earnings shortfalls; they are likely to face an interest rate premium precisely on account of a weak export position. Some relief is available through the International Monetary Fund (IMF)'s compensatory financing facility, but stringent eligibility conditions and limitations upon amounts available are imposed on potential users.

Uncorrected fluctuations in the LDCs' foreign-exchange earnings may retard economic development in several ways.[7] Erratic export earnings complicate public and private planning, interfere

[7]Although the deleterious effect of export-earnings instability on economic development is taken as axiomatic by many writers, careful empirical research has failed to uncover a clear relationship. A standard work in this area is Alasdair I. MacBean, *Export Instability and Economic Development*, Harvard University Press, Cambridge, Mass., 1966. On the basis of his empirical findings, MacBean concludes that the importance of export-earnings instability in retarding development has been overemphasized.

TABLE 2
Developing-Country Commodity Exports Accounting for More than 20% of Total Export Earnings

Country	Export	Percentage of Total Export Earnings, 1975	
Algeria	Petroleum	91	
Bangladesh	Jute	53	
Barbados	Sugar	42	
Bolivia	Tin	41	
	Petroleum	26	
Burma	Rice	44	
	Teak	22	
Burundi	Coffee	87	
Cameroon	Cacao	25	
	Coffee	24	
Central African Republic	Cotton	23	
	Coffee	23	
Chad	Cotton	65	(1974)
Chile	Copper	67	(1974)
Colombia	Coffee	42	
Congo	Petroleum	54	
Costa Rica	Bananas	27	
Dominican Republic	Sugar	65	
Ecuador	Petroleum	57	
Egypt	Cotton	37	
El Salvador	Coffee	33	
Ethiopia	Coffee	31	
Gabon	Petroleum	86	
Gambia	Peanuts	92	
Ghana	Cacao	54	(1974)
Guatemala	Coffee	25	
Guyana	Sugar	50	(1974)
	Bauxite and alumina	32	(1974)

TABLE 2
Developing-Country Commodity Exports Accounting for More than 20% of Total Export Earnings (Cont.)

Country	Export	Percentage of Total Export Earnings, 1975	
Haiti	Coffee	33	
Honduras	Bananas	21	
Indonesia	Petroleum	74	
Iran	Petroleum	97	
Iraq	Petroleum	99	
Ivory Coast	Coffee	24	
Jamaica	Bauxite and alumina	68	
	Sugar	21	
Jordan	Phosphates	41	
Kuwait	Petroleum	93	
Liberia	Iron ore	75	
Libya	Petroleum	100	
Malawi	Tobacco	42	
Malaysia	Rubber	37	
Mauritania	Iron ore	82	
Mauritius	Sugar	85	
Morocco	Phosphates	47	
Nicaragua	Cotton	25	
Nigeria	Petroleum	93	
Panama	Bananas	21	
Philippines	Sugar	26	
	Coconut products	20	
Rwanda	Coffee	63	
Saudi Arabia	Petroleum	100	
Senegal	Phosphates	26	(1974)
	Peanuts	21	(1974)
Sierra Leone	Diamonds	54	
Somalia	Bananas	20	(1974)

TABLE 2
Developing-Country Commodity Exports Accounting for More than 20% of Total Export Earnings (Cont.)

Country	Export	Percentage of Total Export Earnings, 1975	
Sri Lanka	Tea	49	
Sudan	Cotton	46	
	Peanuts	22	
Syria	Petroleum	69	
Togo	Phosphates	76	(1974)
Tunisia	Petroleum	5ʃ	
	Phosphates	20	
Uganda	Coffee	76	
Uruguay	Wool	23	
Venezuela	Petroleum	95	
Western Samoa	Copra	57	
	Cacao	26	
Zaire	Copper	66	(1974)
Zambia	Copper	90	

SOURCE: International Monetary Fund, *International Financial Statistics*, December 1976.

with sound trade and exchange policies, and disrupt imports of capital goods and industrial inputs. Furthermore, given the pervasive rigidities characteristic of most developing economies, export-price upswings can have deleterious effects by exacerbating inflationary pressure.

SECURITY

For commodity importers, a major goal in current negotiations is assured access to required raw-material imports at more stable prices than in the recent past. Because primary commodities—even oil—are far less central to the economies of the industrialized consuming nations than is the case for LDC exporters, individual price fluctuations are not as critical for the consuming as for the producing nations. Also, the wealthier consuming nations are better able to insulate themselves from world markets through a variety of unilateral measures. Nevertheless, large unanticipated price movements have undesired allocative and distributive consequences within the industrialized nations and may contribute to overall inflationary pressures if a "ratchet" mechanism allows domestic prices to follow import costs upward but not downward, as some believe. But for the United States and other industrialized nations, all dependent on imports of at least some key raw materials, a more serious threat is posed by short-term supply interruptions along the lines of the Arab oil embargo.

The oil embargo and subsequent dramatic increases in the price of oil and many other internationally traded commodities during 1974 stimulated most industrialized nations to assess their dependence on imported raw materials. The degree of dependence varies significantly across commodities. As shown in Table 3, developing nations account for a large fraction of total world supply of some metals and of tropical agricultural commodities but for a far smaller fraction of other raw materials, including some important food crops. In addition to growing a large share of world grain supplies, the U.S.S.R. is a major producer of minerals. And among the noncommunist developed countries, the United States, Canada, and Australia together account for a high proportion of world production of many commodities.

While it is relatively straightforward to determine which countries dominate world production of any given primary commodity, patterns of consumption are more difficult to assess. Furthermore, implications of price changes or supply interruptions will be different for importing processors than for ultimate consumers. Most primary commodities pass through several stages of processing before reaching their ultimate destination. For raw materials as diverse as cocoa, iron ore, and petroleum, a typical processing pattern is likely to entail at least three countries: the exporter of the relatively unprocessed raw material, a more industrialized nation somewhat specialized in refining

TABLE 3
Major Primary-Commodity Producers

Commodity	Major Producers, 1974	Output as Percentage of World Total	
		Top Four LDC Producers	All LDCs
Agricultural			
Cocoa	Ghana, Nigeria, Ivory Coast, Brazil, Cameroon, Ecuador	69	100
Coffee	Brazil, Colombia, Ivory Coast, Angola, Uganda, Guatemala	55	100
Corn	U.S., China, Brazil, U.S.S.R., South Africa, France, Yugoslavia, Mexico, Argentina	18	36
Cotton	U.S.S.R., U.S., China, India, Pakistan, Turkey, Brazil	32	63
Jute	India, Bangladesh, China, Burma, Nepal, Thailand	93	100
Peanuts	India, China, U.S., Senegal, Sudan, Nigeria	55	86
Rice	China, India, Indonesia, Bangladesh, Japan, Thailand	67	92
Rubber, Natural	Malaysia, Indonesia, Thailand, Sri Lanka, India, Liberia	85	100
Soybeans	U.S., Brazil, China	30	32
Sugar	U.S.S.R., Brazil, India, Cuba, U.S., France, Mexico	28	32
Tea	India, China, Sri Lanka, Japan, Indonesia, Kenya	67	89
Wheat	U.S.S.R., U.S., China, India, France, Canada	20	30

Wool	Australia, U.S.S.R., New Zealand, Argentina, South Africa, China	14	18
Mineral			
Bauxite	Australia, Jamaica, Guinea, Surinam, U.S.S.R., Guyana	42	53
Copper	U.S., U.S.S.R., Chile, Canada, Zambia, Zaire	32	37
Iron Ore	U.S.S.R., Australia, U.S., Brazil, China, Canada	24	35
Lead	U.S., U.S.S.R., Australia, Canada, Mexico, Peru	18	29
Petroleum	U.S.S.R., U.S., Saudi Arabia, Iran, Venezuela, Kuwait	36	63
Tin	Malaysia, U.S.S.R., Bolivia, Indonesia, Thailand, Australia	62	77
Zinc	Canada, U.S.S.R., U.S., Australia, Peru, Mexico	18	27

SOURCE: *UN Yearbook of Industrial Statistics*, 1974; *UN Statistical Yearbook*, 1975; *FAO Production Yearbook*, 1974; *Commodity Yearbook*, 1976.

activities, and a still more industrialized nation in which cocoa becomes a processed food, steel is embodied in automobiles or construction, and refined oil is used to produce energy (which itself may be an input in the production of other industrial intermediate goods).

Among the major developed nations, the United States relies to a relatively small degree on imported raw materials, although dependence on oil imports has continued to increase in recent years. The European Community imports a larger fraction of its raw materials, and resource-poor Japan depends upon imports for virtually all its needs. A 1975 study by a United States government task force[8] set United States dependence on imports at 15% of total requirements of key raw materials, while the corresponding figures given for Western Europe and Japan were 75 and 90 percent. In recent years the industrialized nations have intensified efforts to diversify import sources and have expressed renewed interest in maintaining stockpiles of those critical commodities that might be attractive targets for future embargo attempts. For many raw materials, substantial government and private stockpiles are already maintained.

Figures for current and projected imports of various commodities tell only part of the story, however. The actual amount obtained from each source and the total amount consumed each year both reflect a given history of past prices and expectations of future prices. A substantial increase in prices charged by foreign producers or in the threat of supply interruptions will automatically reduce dependence on foreign supplies by reducing total consumption through substitution and by increasing domestic supplies from increased production and recycling. Thus, the actual dislocations that would occur in a given commodity market as a result of an important change in price or availability cannot be gleaned easily from summary statistics on present imports, but must take into account the price-responsiveness of alternative supply and of demand. On the other hand, theoretical possibilities of substitution in supply or end use often prove

[8]Quoted in *Council Report*, no. 16, United States–Japan Trade Council, March 12, 1975.

costlier than anticipated, in part because increased demand drives up the prices of required inputs. In the case of oil, substitute coal soared in price, while even a prolonged period of higher oil prices has not brought any significant supplies from oil shale or tar sands, previously seen as important alternative sources.

Less developed exporters of raw materials are keenly aware that consumer dependence may easily be eroded by development of new sources or substitutes. To this consideration some observers attribute the many delays inserted by LDC representatives into internal proceedings on regulation of mineral recovery from the seabeds. The UNCTAD Permanent Group on Synthetics and Substitutes, a subsidiary body of the influential Committee on Commodities, has promoted research and development to delay the encroachment of synthetics into the markets for natural products. Some LDC representatives have even called for taxes or other restraints on the use of synthetic substitutes.

An additional dimension of the security objective concerns the perpetuation of existing international economic relationships. To the extent that failure to reach a compromise on primary commodities drives North and South ever farther apart, destructive sequences of provocation and retaliation become more likely. Not only flows of raw materials but all other North-South trade and investment linkages could be imperiled by commodity-engendered international conflict. While many argue that the nations of the South have relatively more to lose through such an outcome, the potential losses of the industrialized world are nevertheless substantial.

THREE

Alternative Commodity Regimes

Much of the debate on commodity policy has centered upon the appropriate role of market forces. The key issue is thus cast as market versus nonmarket or laissez faire versus government intervention. However, the decision to allow the market to operate freely or, alternatively, to suppress market forces, hinges upon the presumed outcome. In some markets, a policy of laissez faire ensures a result closely approximating the textbook notion of "perfect competition." In other cases, buyers or sellers may be able to exercise a conscious influence over market outcomes, their ability to do so either reinforced or undermined by government policies.

In the following analysis, we have characterized alternative arrangements for world commodity trade in terms of *outcomes* rather than policies. Specifically, our analysis focuses upon the ability of transactors, individually or in groups, to control market outcomes. Thus, we are looking at the interaction of policy choices and underlying market structure in achieving particular outcomes. We envision any actual trading arrangement as comprising some combination of four hypothetical control structures or regimes. These regimes are the competitive market, unilateral producer control, unilateral consumer control, and negotiated control. Each regime accommodates a different (but mutually overlapping) set of policy instruments, and each has some claim to being the most satisfactory means of achieving one or more of the underlying objectives of redistribution, stability, security, and efficiency.

Although the four regimes are ideal types rather than realistic models of economic performance, they provide a useful starting point for analyzing the properties of actual markets for particular commodities. While certain commodity markets do closely resemble one or another of the four regimes, more often elements of two or more regimes are present. Furthermore, since outcomes depend upon both policies and underlying market structure, the same *formal* arrangement can lead to very different outcomes and hence be consistent with two different regimes in our sense. This could be true either for two commodities or for the same commodity at different points in time.

Of the four regimes, the one most often discussed, but only infrequently observed in primary commodity trade, is the competitive market. The hallmark of the competitive market is that producers and consumers alike act individually and are individually powerless to affect world prices in a significant way. The transactions of any seller or buyer must be small relative to the total size of the market. In the competitive market regime, *no* effective control over market outcomes is exercised by any interested party. Any alternative to the competitive market entails some combination of actions on the part of consumers or producers to exercise conscious, collective influence over market outcomes. Such collective control may be implemented through measures that affect world supply, world demand, or both. Three noncompetitive regimes can be identified: *unilateral producer control*, *unilateral consumer control*, and *negotiated control*. While it is impossible to identify real situations that correspond perfectly to these three hypothetical extremes, some actual markets provide reasonable approximations. Unilateral producer control, as typified by OPEC, has been the regime most prominent in recent headlines. The trading arrangements instituted by the imperial powers during the colonial period, with the interests of producing regions largely unrepresented in market decisions, can be used to illustrate unilateral consumer control. Finally, the announced objective of most explicit producer-consumer commodity agreements is the establishment of a world regime of negotiated control. However, as we shall emphasize below, the *formal* participation of both producers and consumers does not ensure that each group will be able to exercise some effective control over the outcome.

In recent decades, control itself, as distinct from the distribution of benefits, has come to be an important issue in North-South negotiations. In discussions of international commodity trade, it is usually implicitly assumed that the parties controlling market outcomes will exercise that control in such a way as to realize the greatest possible benefits for themselves. However, the economic benefits to noncontrolling parties may nonetheless be significant. For example, a powerful producers' alliance might effectively control the market but use that control to produce some benefits for others. Some Arab members of OPEC have earmarked a substantial part of increased export earnings for assistance to non-OPEC Muslim developing countries. Likewise, the imperial exploiters of colonial mineral wealth in some instances allocated large sums to religious, educational, and medical expenditures assumed beneficial to the producing regions. In either case, the benefactors were no doubt motivated by a combination of humanitarian concerns and self-interest, but the possibility of real benefits to noncontrolling parties should not be overlooked.[9] Yet even where controlling interests are unambiguously benevolent in their intent, beneficiaries and donors can differ in their assessment of priorities, and the benevolence of the North is in any case not readily acknowledged by Southern nations. The desire of LDCs to control their own economic and social destinies, rather than to depend upon the largess of the traditional powers, is likely to be a major factor in any new international agreements.

COMPETITIVE MARKETS

Economists since Adam Smith have devoted much of their effort to investigating the properties of competitive markets. The most

[9]Those controlling market outcomes may be viewed as maximizing an interdependent social welfare function that includes arguments other than the group's own economic well-being as narrowly defined. See McCulloch and Piñera, "Trade as Aid," op. cit.

important conclusion emerging from this body of work is that, under suitable conditions, a system of competitive markets will lead to a world allocation of resources which is *efficient* in a specific technical sense:[10] no individual or group can be made better off without leaving another worse off. In other words, the operation of the market eliminates waste or slack from the system. A corollary of this key finding is that competitive markets will also have desirable stability and security properties. With respect to the distribution of benefits, the competitive outcome has no particular relationship to perceived "neediness" of transactors. The distributive impact both within and between nations will depend primarily upon the existing distribution of property rights over natural resources. Nevertheless, a desirable distribution is promoted through two indirect channels. To the extent that greater overall efficiency is achieved, total world wealth available for distribution is increased; a context of growing per capita income is likely to facilitate redistribution from rich to poor. Furthermore, the absence of centralized economic power reduces the ability of already rich and powerful groups within the world economy to futher improve their lot through nonmarket wealth allocations.

Observed commodity market performance falls conspicuously short of the attractive theoretical scenario. There are several explanations for this apparent contradiction. Most important is the confusion in discussions of alternative commodity regimes between competitive markets and situations of laissez faire in which no form of official national or international intervention is imposed. For many commodities, the market shares of individual buyers and sellers may be sufficiently great to enable them to exercise considerable market power. For these commodities, the absence of official intervention merely clears the way for oligopolistic market structures in which a few transactors dominate market outcomes. In terms of our analytical framework,

[10]Although this type of efficiency, also known as "Pareto optimality," is associated with competitive-market outcomes, the same criterion can be applied in the context of central planning.

these markets should therefore be classified as producer-controlled or consumer-controlled rather than competitive. Market control may be exercised through explicit arrangements, such as those that have characterized the world markets for petroleum and tin, or through the looser channel of mutual awareness and implicit coordination. In the cases of commodities including diamonds, gold, oil, tin, copper, rubber, and bananas, individual producers control a substantial share of the market. Likewise, large individual purchasers, whether firms or nations, are often able to exert substantial pressure on market outcomes; the United States and the U.S.S.R. have each demonstrated this potential on many occasions.

Just as laissez faire policies in the domestic economy do not preclude noncompetitive behavior on the part of firms, the absence of international commodity agreements does not preclude noncompetitive behavior by producers or consumers. To *ensure* competitive behavior in primary-commodity markets would require active intervention, specifically an effective international antitrust policy. However, such a policy does not seem feasible in the current atmosphere of increased nationalism, with few countries willing to cede sovereignty to international authorities. Furthermore, experience in the industrialized countries with implementation of existing antitrust legislation reveals the many possible pitfalls of such a policy. Particularly where production is subject to extensive scale economies, as in most mining and some agricultural primary producing activities, restrictions on the size of producing units entails some sacrifice of economic efficiency in production. And where, as in the case of oil, gold, or diamonds, accidents of geography restrict the number of producers to a handful, a competitive-market outcome could be achieved only if each producer adopted an artificial rule to determine output instead of acting in the nation's perceived best interest. Thus, for commodities in which individual producers and consumers exercise considerable market power, laissez faire policies cannot ensure competition and indeed are unlikely to be conducive to it. The laissez faire option may yield results superior to or less desirable than other alternatives, but the case for laissez faire policies cannot be made for these commodities through appeal to the theoretical literature on competitive market performance.

Even when producers and consumers are each sufficiently small that none can individually exercise an appreciable effect on market outcomes, the competitive market may yield results that fall short of the theoretical ideal for other reasons. Among these, perhaps most important is that information is costly to obtain. Thus, transactors will not typically be guided in their buying and selling decisions by full information about technical and commercial possibilities. The less well informed market participants are, the more the outcome will deviate from the optimum.

A second significant reason for suboptimal market performance is that price signals to buyers and sellers may not accurately reflect true underlying economic conditions. Taxation and government regulation are major sources of distorted market signals, causing private costs and returns to differ systematically from their values to society as a whole. Private and social costs and benefits will also differ whenever there are economic "spill-over" effects, such as environmental damage, which are not fully borne by those who generate them.

A crucial area in which inappropriate market signals may arise is the allocation of supplies of exhaustible resources between present and future uses. Critics of the competitive market argue that the interests of future generations are likely to be under-represented in current decisions, leading to excessively rapid depletion of such resources. In technical language, the private rate of discount (of future relative to current benefits and costs) is higher than the correct social rate of discount. No market participants take a sufficiently long view of world economic prospects. On the other hand, imperfect information may lead to an overstatement of the future value of depletable resources by failing to anticipate the development of new sources or substitutes.

Critics of uncontrolled commodity markets have focused their attack on the alleged poor performance of such markets in providing price stability for exporters and supply security for importers, citing the violent price fluctuations and costly supply interruptions characteristic of international commodity markets in recent years. However, commodity markets that have been subject to pervasive control in the past, including markets in sugar, tin, and coffee, have experienced roller-coaster price movements as spectacular as those observed in markets where regulation has played a smaller role. It is thus unclear whether the observed instability and supply disruptions reflect the need for greater control or the perverse effects of existing intervention.

Price fluctuations produced by changes in demand or supply conditions, whatever their cause, represent part of the normal functioning of the market. By signaling relative scarcity or abundance to buyers and sellers, they trigger appropriate demand and supply responses, including changes in privately held inventories of storable commodities. Elimination of price fluctuations also eliminates these responses on the part of profit-seeking individuals. Even the likelihood of official intervention in response to unusual supply or price conditions will depress private stabilization activity below its socially desirable level. Private holders of scarce primary commodities do not expect to be able to capture the full economic value of speculatively held stocks at times of scarcity and high prices. Likewise, if national or international action is likely to insulate producers from the full effects of unusually low prices, producers will have weakened incentives to diversify their outputs or to shift production toward commodities with relatively low price variance (which will in turn create a price differential to reward producers willing to supply relatively risky commodities). Thus, observed price fluctuations may not reflect the defects of competition so much as the result of erratic regulatory activities on the national or international level.[11] Nevertheless, as long as modern governments and in-

---

[11] Proponents of freer markets stress the potential stabilizing effects of private transactions. However, some observers believe that actions of private speculators may be destabilizing. By buying in anticipation of still higher prices in the near future, rather than selling in anticipation of lower prices in the more distant future, private speculators may amplify short-term price fluctuations. In their analysis of the 1972–1975 commodity-price boom, R. N. Cooper and R. Z. Lawrence stress the role of speculative purchases. See R. N. Cooper

ternational organizations retain a mandate for action of this type, the desirability of the competitive market as a means of organizing international exchange of primary commodities will be undermined to some extent.

CONTROLLED MARKETS

The competitive market is characterized by the absence of control over outcomes on the part of any market participant; alternatives to the competitive market necessarily entail the exercise of effective control by some buyers or sellers acting individually or in concert. Although the three possible control configurations—unilateral producer control, unilateral consumer control, negotiated control—differ in significant respects, the underlying problems and techniques of control are similar. Furthermore, the same *formal* structure, such as a producer-consumer commodity agreement or a vertically integrated multinational firm, can be consistent with any one of the three regimes.

Buffer-stock arrangements have played a prominent role in past and present efforts to control commodity trade. Depending upon the method of operation, buffer stocks can be used to achieve unilateral control by producers or consumers, or negotiated control. Buffer stocks affect the market price of storable commodities by removing supply from the market when price is low and augmenting market supply when price is high. A central authority is empowered to make appropriate sales and purchases. Typically, floor and ceiling prices are negotiated; a market price at or below the floor triggers purchases by the central authority, while a price at or above the ceiling is a signal to sell to the market. The result is to moderate price fluctuations and, depending on the target prices set, perhaps also to raise or lower average price. The ability of the buffer to moderate downward fluctuations or to resist a longer-term trend in price depends on the size of the fund available for buffer accumulation. Like-

---

and R. Z. Lawrence, "The 1972–75 Commodity Boom," *Brookings Papers on Economic Activity*, vol. 3, 1975, pp. 671–723.

wise, the size of the stock itself determines the extent to which the arrangement can moderate price rises in times of short supply.[12]

A useful distinction can be made between control that is exercised *through* the market and that which *supplants* the market. Pure monopoly or monopsony, in which the market is dominated by a single large seller or buyer, with all other participants having negligible market shares, is the most obvious case of control exercised through the market. More complex arrangements that operate through market forces include taxes or subsidies and buffer stocks. In these cases, individual participants pursue their own interests, as in a competitive setting; what differs is the system of incentives to which transactors respond. In contrast, market-supplanting arrangements eliminate the market function of resource allocation for some transactions and substitute direct controls over sales or purchases.[13]

While most commodity arrangements include elements of both types of control, the distinction between the exercise of economic power through the market and its use to supplant the market has important implications for the viability of a desired outcome. Where control is exercised through the market, the system is self-enforcing in the sense that buyers and sellers are permitted to act in their own best interests as individually perceived. Market-supplanting devices create incentives for individual transactors to act in ways that tend to undermine the desired outcome; long-term enforcement of such arrangements is likely to be expensive and cumbersome.

The ultimate goals of market control will be some combination of the four discussed above—redistribution, efficiency, stability, security—but all are achieved through control over market price or quantity. It is important to recognize (as many of those at-

---

[12]The International Tin Agreement, which has used a buffer arrangement, succeeded to some extent in smoothing small price fluctuations but was unable to resist larger price movements.

[13]Monopoly often results from noneconomic barriers to entry, particularly government restriction. This case is better characterized as market-supplanting, since it would be in the interest of other suppliers to enter the market if they were not prevented from doing so.

tempting to establish commodity agreements apparently do not) that successful market control does not permit both price *and* quantity to be determined arbitrarily.[14] Those exercising market power are constrained in their actions by the behavior of all remaining market participants.

UNILATERAL PRODUCER CONTROL

The simplest example of market control is pure monopoly: a single seller facing many independent buyers. Monopoly represents an extreme case of unilateral producer control, seldom observed in any real market. It is important, however, because it is the model toward which *any* arrangement for unilateral producer control is likely to strive. A cartel—a group of producers acting in concert—can do no better than to emulate the monopolist's market strategy, to act as a single seller would. But only rarely will this ideal be achieved, for as long as more than a single seller serves the market, the interests of any one supplier will differ systematically from those of the group.

In contrast to a small supplier, the monopolist takes into account the induced effect on market price and knows that the larger the total quantity supplied to the market, the lower the price at which this quantity can be sold. Alternatively, if the monopolist sets a price, the higher the price, the smaller the quantity required to satisfy all potential purchasers. The monopolist thus faces a *demand schedule* determined by the behavior of buyers (and perhaps also of smaller suppliers). This demand schedule gives all price-quantity combinations that will clear the market. From these alternative combinations, the monopolist seeks the one that best achieves a chosen objective, typically the maximization of total profits.

The monopolist's profit-maximizing choice is complicated by incomplete information. In practice the demand schedule is never known with certainty. Thus, the seller may set a price, only to

[14]Problems encountered in centrally planned economies often reflect an attempt to set both price and quantity. The result is likely to be a shortage or a glut and, sometimes, illegal transactions.

find that the total demanded by consumers is less (or more) than expected. However, a far greater source of uncertainty concerns future market conditions. The monopolist does not maximize today's profits without regard to future profits, but rather seeks to maximize the *present discounted value* of profits, both current and future, with future profits appropriately adjusted to take account of the rate of interest and the uncertainty of future market conditions.

The monopolist's current actions may affect future profits through two quite different channels. First, where the commodity can be stored—particularly in the case of exhaustible resources—the monopolist will time sales in such a way that total anticipated profits cannot be increased by storing more or less for sale at a future date. This means, for example, that the expected *reduction* in total profits from a small reduction in scheduled sales for 1979 must just offset the expected *increase* in total profits from an equal increase in scheduled sales for 1980. The required calculation takes account not only of the effect on revenues in each year but also of the cost of storage for one year and the appropriate rate of discount required to make a 1979 and a 1980 receipt comparable. The members of OPEC are reported to have discussed calculations of this type in deciding how much oil to supply in a given year.

A second way the monopolist's current actions may affect future profits is through induced effects on future supply and demand schedules. A high current price promotes entry by new suppliers as well as consumer search for alternative means of satisfying a particular need. The high price of coffee maintained by Brazil during the early decades of the century brought many new suppliers into the market, eroding Brazil's near-monopoly position. Likewise, the dramatic post-1973 increase in the price of oil stimulated much ultimately successful exploration that would not have been undertaken at the earlier price; sharply increased prices also sent energy consumers in search of alternatives such as coal, nuclear power, and solar energy. The monopolist may take these kinds of responses into account by choosing a price low enough to deter some erosion of his or her market power through new entry or substitution. However, because such responses are highly uncertain, the monopolist's behavior may be affected only slightly by these considerations.

The monopolist's profit-maximizing strategy need not entail charging a single price to all buyers. If the monopolist is able to effectively separate the market into segments with different demand characteristics—different price-responsiveness or elasticity—profits can be further enhanced through *price discrimination* among buyers. Buyers with low price elasticity of demand will be charged a higher price than those who are more price-responsive. Obviously, market segmentation cannot be maintained if low-price customers are able to resell their purchases in the higher-price markets. Price discrimination is therefore facilitated by high transport costs or inflexible transport networks, such as pipelines. It is also easier to discriminate among buyers if the product occurs in many grades or types that are viewed by users as imperfect substitutes, as in the cases of coffee, rice, and petroleum.

The above discussion assumes that the monopolist's goal is to maximize profits or, more precisely, to maximize the present discounted value of profits. This is an appropriate goal for a monopolist who has ready access to capital markets. If the monopolist's desired pattern of expenditures over time does not match the pattern of receipts implied by profit maximization, lending and borrowing transactions can accommodate the divergences. But if the seller is not viewed as creditworthy—a problem for many less developed countries—some sacrifice of total profits may be chosen in order to provide sufficient revenues to meet current needs. Also, a monopolist viewing capital-market lending opportunities as risky for economic or political reasons may wish to "invest" instead in stockpiles of his or her own commodity.

A related question is whether a risk premium, *over* the market rate of interest, ought to be incorporated into the monopolist's present value calculations—i.e., whether future profits should be discounted because of their greater uncertainty as well as because of their later occurrence in time. The current approach of economists to this question centers on the monopolist's ability to eliminate this risk through portfolio diversification, that is, by purchase of other assets that have complementary risk characteristics. If such assets are available, the monopolist can choose how much risk to bear. But if such diversification is not available, inclusion of a risk premium is indicated. In this case, the monopolist's objective may be to stabilize, as well as to raise, the market price.

If a cartel or producers' organization is viewed as a monopolist with more than one production facility, maximization of total profits entails the allocation of output among facilities in such a way as to minimize total cost. Then, given the total cost schedule for alternative levels of supply, the profit-maximizing price-quantity combination is chosen. The precise condition for minimization of total cost is that each facility's production level be selected so that cost *at the margin* is the same for all. Some higher-cost facilities may be shut down completely.[15] This cost-minimization problem is straightforward when all production facilities are owned by a single supplier. In a cartel, the problem becomes more complex. An efficient allocation of production among cartel members can be achieved through a uniform export tax. However, the resulting contractions of member output will depend upon individual cost structures. If cost structures differ, cost minimization may be achieved with lower-cost producers supplying the bulk of the total, while higher-cost producers supply little or nothing. To induce the latter to accept the efficient allocation of production, "side payments" would be required; i.e., the producers supplying large amounts would assign part of their sales receipts to higher-cost producers. The division of total cartel profits among producers with different cost structures is thus an obvious source of disagreement. For this reason, a producers' organization may opt for a somewhat inefficient allocation of production and lower total profits, allow each country to retain the revenues generated by its own sales, and thus eliminate or at least moderate the role of side payments.

[15]This "corner solution" to the problem of cost minimization is most likely to occur when cost configurations for alternative sources differ markedly. However, even if all facilities have the same costs, it may be efficient to shut down one or more facilities to eliminate high fixed overhead costs of operation.

A theoretical alternative to the uniform export tax as a means of achieving an efficient allocation of production among cartel members is a system of marketable export quotas. These quotas may be allocated in any agreed fashion among members. The initial allocation need not take individual cost structures into account. For higher-cost producers, the value from sale of export rights to other producers will tend to exceed the profits from exercising the rights directly. Thus, the result could be equivalent to that achieved through a uniform export tax and side payments. However, given a relatively small number of cartel members, a bilateral monopoly situation would emerge between high-cost and low-cost producers, thus introducing another potential source of conflict within the cartel.

However production shares are designated, the cartel's central problem is to enforce these shares. Individual seller production may be controlled through the use of export taxes or through assignment of export quotas. Export taxes actually modify the sellers' incentives, so that it is no longer in their individual interests to supply an excessive quantity. However, each member nation still faces the incentive to reduce its tax or give its producers other special treatment in order to expand the nation's market share. Export taxes have been used successfully in the case of petroleum by OPEC members. They have also been employed by bauxite producers in an attempt to raise world price.

Production or export quotas work best when production is concentrated among a few countries and is centrally controlled within those countries (diamonds provide the classic example of effective control of price through supply restriction) and when production cutbacks are accompanied by minimal internal dislocations in employment, as with petroleum. Where one seller or a small group of sellers controls a large fraction of total production, only the production of the dominant supplier(s) need be controlled directly; the dominant producer supplies the *difference* between world demand at the target price and the amount that remaining sellers would normally wish to supply at that price. In the markets for oil and coffee, this arrangement has been characteristic. As production from all sources responds to the elevated price, however, the dominant supplier receives a shrinking share of total revenues and thus may choose to abandon the price umbrella, as Brazil did in the case of coffee.

With many sellers of nonnegligible size, allocation of production or export quotas becomes a major stumbling block in controlling total supply. Formulas based on cost or capacity considerations may yield temporary agreement, but since some or perhaps all sellers can produce additional amounts at costs well below the prevailing cartel price, the incentives to exceed quotas are strong. If an appreciable number of producers respond to these individual incentives, market control will be undermined. Furthermore, an effective cartel is likely to promote new entrants. If new suppliers remain outside the group, these late arrivals are able to sell at or near the cartel price, achieving their own profits at the cost of the cartel members. Even if the new entrants are brought into the producers' association, the profits of the original members will be eroded and any compromise previously reached on the division of profits must be renegotiated. Thus, the very success of a cartel may be the source of its ultimate demise.

For commodities that can be stored at reasonable cost, an alternative approach to unilateral producer control is a buffer stock. Unlike production or export quotas and export taxes, the operation of a buffer stock requires funding. Obviously, a buffer arrangement with the limited objective of smoothing price fluctuations by augmenting private transactions[16] carries a far smaller price tag than a buffer intended to raise average price as well. In the latter case, continuously growing stocks and financing requirements are inevitable, and support for the arrangement may be difficult to maintain. A buffer stock and export controls may be used together to raise and stabilize price.[17] To the extent they are effective, the export controls will reduce the total financial cost (and accompanying stock accumulation) that would

[16]A buffering arrangement that succeeded in moderating price fluctuations might actually lower average price over time to the extent that stable prices induced additional suppliers to enter the market.

[17]Although the Tin Agreement is usually described as a buffer-stock arrangement, export controls have been imposed on a regular basis to supplement buffering during periods of price decline.

be otherwise required to maintain the price through buffer purchases alone.

The implications of unilateral producer control for the four objectives identified above depend crucially upon the success and longevity of the arrangement. Effective market control maintained over a long period is most probable in the case of true monopoly, e.g., South African diamond production. The erosion of monopoly power through development of alternative sources and through substitution in consumption is likely to be a slow process, extending over years or even decades. This means that the monopoly producer can be assured of the desired "mix" of profits (redistribution) and earnings stability. Implications for consumer security are less clear, as the monopolist may choose to use economic power for political ends. It should be noted, however, that doing this entails a compromise of the monopolist's own economic objectives. When this appears to be a significant threat, consumers may take political or even military action to gain control over the monopolized resource.

The exercise of monopoly power is likely to result in a lower level of world economic efficiency than if the same market were served by many independent suppliers. The nature of the efficiency loss is the restriction of world production and consumption below its optimal level as measured by social costs and benefits. If, however, there is a divergence between private and social costs and benefits, market signals to producers and consumers will be inappropriate. In particular, if the time rate of discount used by producers and consumers is higher than the appropriate rate for society as a whole, the monopolist's restriction of output, while motivated by purely private goals, could nonetheless raise world welfare by conserving exhaustible resources that would otherwise be depleted too rapidly.

The consequences of a long-lived cartel are similar to those of a pure monopoly. The major differences arise from the cartel's problem of reconciling cost minimization with division of profits among members. Any compromise required to accommodate higher-cost producers will mean a further loss of world efficiency beyond that resulting from restriction of total output; higher-cost producers are likely to derive a larger *share* of total profits under such an arrangement than in the absence of producer control.

It is, however, improbable that a cartel will be as durable as a pure monopoly. Cartel control is more susceptible to disruption since some or all producers face individual incentives to increase supply, thus tending to undermine the arrangement. A sustained price increase will also attract new entrants, eroding the profits of the original group. A cartel that relies primarily upon market-supplanting techniques of control, such as production or export quotas, will be more vulnerable to disruption from within than one in which market-supplementing devices actually alter the incentives faced by individual sellers. But even with market-supplementing devices the cartel structure is likely to be unstable. In a buffer-stock arrangement, stability may be undermined if the central authority lacks the resources required to resist price movements outside the designated limits. Furthermore, if there is doubt as to the adequacy of these resources, speculators will add to the buffer's task by purchasing larger amounts as the market price approaches the designated ceiling and selling from inventories as the price falls toward the floor. A more remote but more serious possibility is that organization by sellers to raise price or restrict supply may provoke economic, political, or military retaliation by consumers.

Higher commodity prices brought about by cartelization of supply alter the distribution of wealth between North and South, among the nations of the South, and within individual producer nations. As noted in Chapter 2, an increase in commodity prices, particularly for an appropriately chosen subset rather than for all commodities, will redistribute income from North to South, although not necessarily from rich to poor. Among the nations of the South, distribution of such gains is largely arbitrary; in the absence of intra-South foreign aid, those nations with most to gain from cartelization of commodity exports are not necessarily those with greatest need as measured in terms of per capita income. On the contrary, many of the poorest nations are commodity importers.

The distribution of gains among the members of a particular cartel and within a given member nation depends crucially upon the methods used by the cartel to achieve the required contraction of world supply. Distribution of gains among cartel members is determined primarily by the shares in total output allocated to

145

each and by whatever side payments or transfers, if any, are made. Within a given nation, the gains from a higher price may accrue initially to the government rather than to individual suppliers. In this case, the actual incidence of gains depends upon the way in which the revenues are spent; in particular, producers need not benefit.

If an export tax is the mechanism used to restrict output, suppliers will receive a net price that differs from the world price by the amount of the tax. For the required reduction in output to be achieved, the net price received by suppliers must necessarily be *lower* than the precartel price. Lower price and production levels may have further distributive consequences through payments by suppliers for labor, land, and other inputs. When producers' incomes are already low, as in the case of small-scale growers of agricultural commodities, an export tax may not be feasible because of the implied reduction of growers' earnings. This reduction is likely to be deemed undesirable on political or equity grounds, and compensatory transfer payments for those affected are cumbersome to administer. For this reason, a system of quotas may be a preferred method of restricting exports in some cases. If export quotas are allocated to producers, these in effect allow the producers themselves to collect the implicit tax on exports.[18] Export quotas could also be sold to producers, with effects similar to those of an export tax. Alternatively, some fraction of the profits of quota recipients could be taxed away.

An unsuccessful attempt at cartelization may leave all market participants, including the erstwhile cartel members, worse off than under competitive market conditions. The demise of a producers' cartel is likely to be followed by a period of heightened price instability. If individual suppliers have stockpiled output that they were prevented from selling earlier, this accumulation may now be released to the market. Also, an initial period of cartel success is likely to have attracted some new entrants who

---

[18]Competition among producers for valuable export quotas may entail a further misallocation of resources. The effects of "rent-seeking" behavior are discussed in Anne O. Krueger, "The Political Economy of the Rent-Seeking Society," *American Economic Review*, vol. 64, June 1974, pp. 291–303.

would not have found production profitable at the precartel price. These marginal suppliers may continue to operate for a considerable period following the cartel's demise, particularly if production requires large fixed investments. Thus, the average competitive price may be depressed for a number of years until higher-cost producers are forced out. Even a successful cartel may eventually lower the average price received by its members below that which would have prevailed under competition if the high price stimulates fruitful exploration for new mineral resources or development of substitutes, such as synthetic rubber and industrial diamonds.

UNILATERAL CONSUMER CONTROL

The purely technical aspects of market control by a single dominant consumer (monopsony) or by many consumers organized to coordinate their actions are very similar to those of producer control. However, this symmetry does not extend to the objectives of control. Demand for primary commodities is typically inelastic, i.e., unresponsive to price. This means that producers' profits depend crucially on price, so that higher average price is likely to be the principal objective underlying producer control. To the extent that producers' access to capital markets is inadequate to permit desired smoothing of revenue fluctuations over time, a secondary objective may be the stabilization of price around its long-term trend. For consumers, security of supply is the principal objective of market control. Most primary commodities become inputs into complex industrial processes with little scope for short-run substitution. Furthermore, the cost of raw-material inputs is only a fraction, typically a small fraction, of total cost of production of the consumers' own final outputs. Therefore, in terms of total profitability a supply interruption is likely to be far more costly than even a dramatic rise in price. It is for these reasons that consumers' demand is relatively unresponsive to price changes, particularly over short time periods. Obviously consumers will prefer a low price to a higher one, but it is security of supply rather than low average price that is likely

147

to be the primary objective of market control by consumers. Of course, some degree of supply (and price) security can be achieved, at least in the short run, through the use of inventories and futures-market transactions. These measures have been used routinely by most industrial consumers as supplements to direct market control. And for the consuming nation, supply security can also be achieved through measures to stimulate domestic production of key raw materials. It should be noted, however, that national stockpiles or increased national production do not necessarily ensure supply security for an individual consuming enterprise. This depends crucially upon national policies regarding the allocation of these supplies.[19]

Consumer control over primary-commodity markets has taken two major forms. The colonial ties of industrialized nations were motivated in large part by the need to assure supplies of primary inputs as well as markets for finished products. More recently, vertical integration—ownership of primary-commodity sources by industrial consumers—has been a widespread practice of multinational corporations. Vertical integration has been particularly important in the extractive industries, such as aluminum, copper, and tin, where large required initial investments and economies of scale pose economic barriers to entry. The international oil companies have encompassed the full production cycle from extraction of crude oil to retail sales of refined products. However, vertical integration need not extend over this full range of activities. In some industries, a more typical pattern is the vertical linking of primary production and some degree of processing.

Although the activities of vertically integrated multinational firms have been characterized as a form of consumer control, the interests actually served may change over time. In the case of the giant integrated oil companies—some actually owned wholly or in part by consuming nations—managements which were initially responsive only to consumer needs have gradually come to be highly responsive to the desires of the producing

---

[19]As the 1978 United States coal strike demonstrated, even domestic sources may be subject to disruptive supply interruptions.

nations. In such instances, the same group of firms may control the market for an extended period, but with the implications for the underlying objectives of control changing significantly over time. For this reason, the activities of vertically integrated multinational firms may in some cases be more appropriately considered as a form of negotiated control.

Although the motivation for "backward" vertical integration is to ensure a reliable source of required primary inputs, this does not mean that vertical integration is always the best way to achieve supply security. A firm may sometimes be better ensured against supply interruptions through long-term contracts with a number of primary producers in different locations than through ownership of a single source. In the latter case, supply can be disrupted as a result of political difficulties, particularly nationalization, or by such natural occurrences as adverse weather conditions. Long-term contracts with individual producers may thus be considered a third type of consumer control arrangement, depending upon the terms of the contract. But as in the case of vertical integration, the same formal structure is also consistent with a negotiated-control regime.

Consumer control has also been exercised in some markets for key primary commodities through the inventory purchases and sales of important consumers—formal or informal buffer stocks. As part of its international monetary arrangements, the United States stabilized the world price of gold at $35 an ounce between 1934 and 1971 by standing ready to buy or sell gold at that price. Large stockpiles of strategic raw materials, such as tin, have allowed the United States to exercise an important unilateral influence on the world markets for these commodities.

As in the case of producer cartels, market control by consumers may be undermined by conflicting incentives of the participants; the probable reason for breakdown, however, is less likely to be conflict among consumers competing for resources than conflict between consumers and producers over the distribution of gains from market control. The major past instances of consumer control, colonial rule and investment by multinational firms, have been accompanied by many examples of spectacular and disruptive breakdown—revolution and expro-

149

priation. In the case of long-term contracts, breakdown is less likely to be spectacular; producers or consumers may simply refuse to meet the terms of the contract. Legal enforcement of the terms of such contracts is difficult, particularly for international transactions.

Most buffer stocks, whether managed by producers, consumers, or a group including both, soon collapse as a result of insufficient resources. Although the United States' pegging of the dollar price of gold was an instrument of international monetary policy rather than commodity policy, the American experience amply illustrates the potential costliness of buffer-stock arrangements and their vulnerability to changes in underlying economic conditions. When the official price of gold was set by the United States at $35 in 1934, this exceeded the world market-clearing price. As a result, the United States added to its gold stocks for a number of years. Eventually, however, the market-clearing price rose above $35. United States gold stocks began to diminish; as it became clear that America would be forced to change the official price, speculative pressure added to the demand for gold at $35. United States sales of gold at the fixed price were first restricted and finally abandoned.

In terms of the possible objectives served by market control, the successful exercise of market power by consumers is likely to promote security for the consumers themselves and stability for producers. However, since consumer control usually means a lower price to producers, the distribution of gains between consumers and producers is likely to be viewed as inequitable or at least unsatisfactory by the latter. While investments by multinational firms in producing regions have undoubtedly brought about favorable economic developments in the affected regions,[20] it is equally certain that the accompanying level of redistribution (from rich to poor) has been far below that considered desirable by most Southern observers as well as some disinterested Northerners.

As in the case of producer control, aggregate benefits to con-

---

[20]Even colonial rule is believed by many economists to have brought substantial net benefits to Southern areas.

suming nations may conceal important internal redistributive effects. Where control over supplies by oligopolistic industrial consumers allows those firms to exercise monopoly power in the market for processed outputs, ultimate consumers may actually pay higher, rather than lower, prices. Likewise, if a consuming nation exercises monopoly power through a tariff on imports,[21] domestic consumers pay a higher price as a result. The ultimate consequences for distribution depend upon the way in which the tariff revenue is used. If imports are restricted by a quota, the distributive consequences depend on the way in which import licenses are allocated.

The efficiency consequences of consumer control arise from three quite separate considerations. First, a successful control attempt may reduce uncertainty for all participants, thus allowing a possible efficiency gain. This is likely to be the case in voluntary producer-consumer contracts.[22] If unsuccessful attempts to control the market are actually disruptive in their consequences, efficiency will be accordingly reduced. A second consideration arises from the problem of access to capital markets. When potential producers are unable to finance development of raw-material sources, consuming nations or firms may provide the necessary capital in exchange for control over the resulting production. The third aspect of consumer control is its role in reducing competition. Particularly in the case of vertical integration of extractive multinationals, consumer control of primary input sources has facilitated oligopolistic control over the industry's processed *outputs*, thus entailing a likely reduction in world allocative efficiency.

NEGOTIATED CONTROL

The foregoing analysis suggests that, in many markets, laissez faire policies do not ensure free competition. On the contrary,

---

[21]On the theory of "optimum" tariffs to exploit monopoly power, see Harry G. Johnson, "Optimum Tariffs and Retaliation," chap. II in *International Trade and Economic Growth*, Harvard University Press, Cambridge, Mass., 1967.

[22]Such contracts may also be vehicles for negotiated control.

the absence of official restraints on commodity trade merely facilitates actual or attempted market control by producers or by consumers. But such unilateral arrangements are inherently unstable, weakened by the conflicting incentives of the participants. Furthermore, unilateral arrangements by their very nature are not structured to promote overall economic efficiency. These considerations suggest that negotiated control could provide a superior course for all concerned. Ideally, negotiated control over commodity markets would increase economic efficiency. Also, the active participation of both producers and consumers would ensure the viability of the arrangement. But in fact, global efficiency has not been a primary objective in any existing or proposed negotiated control arrangement. Also, the formal participation of both producers and consumers does little to alleviate underlying structural conflicts.

One form of negotiated control—private contractual arrangements between producers and consumers—is already an important feature of the markets for many primary commodities. Negotiated market control cannot be distinguished from producer or consumer control on the basis of formal structure alone. Long-term producer-consumer contracts or foreign direct investments by vertically integrated multinational enterprises may serve primarily the objectives of producers, those of consumers, or some mix of the two. The terms of such arrangements reflect the relative bargaining power of the participants; a situation best characterized as negotiated rather than unilateral control emerges when both sides have comparable bargaining power. As noted earlier, the same formal structure—e.g., the vertically integrated multinational firm—may serve primarily the interests of the consumers at one time and of the producers at a later time. In the extractive industries, where large fixed investments are typically financed by multinational firms, the balance of power between the firms and the producing regions shifts as the required investments are made.

Privately concluded contractual arrangements between producers and consumers are likely to emphasize the stability and security objectives. Price will be set as a compromise between the interests of the parties, with a higher price reflecting greater bargaining strength on the part of producers. The desire of intermediate consumers for lower prices does not typically depend upon the markets for their own outputs; lower input prices mean higher profits for any level of output. However, if the consumers' own output price is regulated or if the consumer is a government agency, incentives to bargain for low input prices may be weak or absent.

Although contractual arrangements between Southern producers and Northern consumers are an important determinant of the current level and distribution of world wealth, existing and proposed international commodity agreements have been far more conspicuous in recent North-South conflicts. International commodity agreements differ from private contractual arrangements in two ways. First, the agreement is among nations rather than among supplying and consuming firms. Of course, the negotiating position of any nation is likely to reflect commercial interests both within and outside that nation. Second, commodity agreements are often concluded within the institutional setting of an international organization such as UNCTAD. This institutional setting may be important to the success of the agreement if it assures the resources required to finance the arrangement or if it increases the likelihood of compliance by members. On the other hand, negotiation within an international organization and particularly within UNCTAD greatly increases the likelihood of issue linkages that complicate the problem of reaching agreement. Furthermore, the very decision to negotiate within an international organization may signal past difficulties in reaching agreement through less formal means.

Two basic types of international commodity agreements may be distinguished on the basis of their primary objectives. *Redistributive* commodity agreements are devised primarily to transfer real resources from Northern importers to Southern exporters. *Stabilizing* commodity agreements are designed primarily to moderate short-term fluctuations around the long-term trend. Although international commodity agreements are highly complex in their specific terms, the control structures established by such agreements are similar to those discussed in previous sections. The major difference is the active participation of both producing and consuming nations.

Redistributive commodity agreements typically rely upon

some combination of export restrictions, producer-consumer contracts governing future transactions, and buffer stocks. The effects of these measures have been discussed above. However, the consequences of formal commodity agreements may differ in certain ways from the effects of similar structures established through other means. Producers are likely to seek a redistributive commodity agreement when unilateral producer control of the market is difficult to sustain. Thus, a commodity agreement might be required to raise prices when a market is served by many suppliers or if entry is relatively easy. These circumstances would apply most readily to agricultural primary commodities, such as sugar, cocoa, coffee, and fibers. The formal participation of consumers in the arrangement reduces the ability of individual suppliers to exceed their designated output quotas by eliminating the market for extra output. Likewise, the ability of new entrants—not parties to the agreement, at least initially—to benefit from the elevated price is lessened. But just as a cartel may eventually be destroyed through conflicts over market shares, an international commodity agreement intended to raise price will be weakened by the continuing need to accommodate new entrants attracted by the higher market price.

As noted earlier, a pure buffer-stock arrangement intended to raise price requires a substantial commitment of resources in order to succeed. In contrast, export restriction through taxation or through the sale of export licenses actually generates resources. For example, if a uniform commodity export tax were levied by an international agency and rebated to LDC exporters, a gross North-South redistributive effect would result. In addition, some portion of the revenues collected would be available to finance grant aid or soft loans to the poorest nations. Of course, the choice of criteria for allocation of such funds would become a potential focus of contention among the members.

Recent negotiations between North and South have focused upon the redistributive implications of commodity trade. Nevertheless, the stability objective has remained important. Stabilizing commodity agreements may employ butter stocks or an export-earnings-stabilization fund. The latter differs from the other measures discussed in that no control over market outcomes is required for success in its operation. An export-earnings-stabilization facility is essentially a lending agency that provides funds to eligible countries on the basis of a shortfall of export earnings below their long-term trend level. In principle, funds borrowed would be restored to the facility if export earnings rose above the calculated trend, thus replenishing funds available for lending.[23]

Export earnings may be stabilized on a commodity-by-commodity basis, for all primary-commodity exports, or for all exports. The Lomé Convention, a comprehensive trade and aid agreement between the European Community (EC) and more than 50 African, Caribbean, and Pacific (ACP) developing nations, provides funds for commodity-by-commodity stabilization of export earnings generated by sales to the EC (Stabex). The International Monetary Fund has established an export-earnings-stabilization facility that limits eligibility to those nations whose overall balance of payments is in deficit as a result of commodity export-earnings shortfalls. Commodity-by-commodity stabilization obviously requires the largest commitment of resources, overall stabilization the smallest. However, the overall criterion used by the IMF in effect penalizes precisely those countries that have made successful attempts to diversify their economies and to expand nontraditional exports. On the other hand, commodity-by-commodity stabilization reduces incentives for LDCs to diversify, and stabilization of overall commodity export earnings reduces incentives for expansion of manufactured exports. But because it provides no protection from an adverse long-term price trend, export-earnings stabilization even on a commodity-by-commodity basis does not completely eliminate incentives for export diversification.

The Stabex and IMF stabilization facilities differ in another important respect, namely, the "normal" earnings level relative to which shortfalls are measured. Under Stabex, compensatory payments are made only if earnings fall short of their average over the four preceding years. Thus, a fall relative to trend for

<hr />

[23]The fund might not be replenished in full, however, if some commodities were subject to a declining long-term price trend.

a growing economy need not generate compensation. In contrast, the IMF scheme measures shortfalls relative to a five-year average centered in the current year.

As in the case of higher export prices, the benefits from earnings stabilization will not necessarily go to the poorest LDCs. For this reason, a per capita income criterion or other "need" basis could be used to limit eligibility. Alternatively, the interest charged on stabilization loans could range from zero for the poorest nations to an appropriate market rate for relatively prosperous nations.

One major focus of recent North-South negotiations has been the UNCTAD proposal for an "integrated program" to restructure world trade in commodities. The integrated program, initially envisioned as covering a list of 18 products (bananas, bauxite, cocoa, coffee, copper, cotton, hard fibers, iron ore, jute, manganese, meat, phosphates, rubber, sugar, tea, tropical timber, tin, and vegetable oils), is intended to raise and stabilize export earnings of LDC producers and to increase the degree of processing in the producing countries. If implemented, the integrated program would mark an important departure from the commodity-by-commodity approach that has characterized previous international arrangements and is still preferred by the United States and most other industrialized consumer nations.

As originally set forth, the integrated program consisted of five elements: creation of buffer stocks for about 10 storable commodities, financing of the buffer-stock operation through a "common fund" to which both producers and consumers would be expected to contribute, improved and expanded export-earnings stabilization, long-term supply and purchase agreements, and expansion of processing in less developed producing nations. However, subsequent negotiations concerning the integrated program have focused primarily upon the proposed establishment of buffer stocks and the common fund. The major points of disagreement between North and South have concerned the size and management of the common fund. Because the common fund would be available to support the price of any one of the 10 buffer-stock commodities, administrators of a large fund would wield considerable power in world markets.

At the end of 1977, LDC negotiators were asking for a common fund of $6 billion and a major role in its management. Northern representatives rejected both the proposed sum, a large part of which would have to be "contributed" by Northern consumer nations, and operating arrangements considered to be dominated by the South. The industrialized countries did offer to pool all resources committed to existing and future agreements for individual commodities, but the LDCs rejected this as inadequate.

Although the integrated program does not make explicit the way in which target price levels would be determined, the Group of 77 initially called for stabilization at levels that take "full account of the rate of world inflation." Taken literally, this would be a proposal for indexation of commodity prices. A later compromise wording omitted the word "full" from the text but left open the extent to which an indexation approach would be attempted. The idea of linking prices of primary commodities to those of the industrialized goods LDC producers must import is a venerable one. The indexation proposal finds its roots in the well-established belief that there is a long-run tendency for the terms of trade to turn against countries exporting primary products. Empirical evidence has not lent clear support to a long-run adverse terms-of-trade movement, but neither has it conclusively demonstrated the opposite. The early 1970s saw soaring prices for almost all raw materials, although most prices subsequently fell to levels well below the highs reached during the 1972–1974 period. A group of UNCTAD experts, commissioned by Secretary-General Gamani Corea to assist in evaluating the indexation proposal, reported in May 1975 that they found no conclusive evidence that developing nations have suffered from adverse long-term price movements. However, even within the group of experts some dissent from this conclusion was expressed.

Whatever the evidence on price movements, indexation is essentially a method of designating target prices rather than a method of maintaining those prices in the face of conflicting market forces. Establishing a relative price that is independent of supply and demand conditions results in a glut or shortage. For those commodities that would otherwise be subject to a declining price trend, continuing inventory accumulation or

157

strictly enforced export limitations would be required to maintain the indexed price. Furthermore, it is unlikely that producers of raw materials experiencing strong world demand would agree to limit their price increases to those dictated by the indexation formula; if they were to do so, shortages would result. Thus, an indexation formula would probably be followed only for commodities with a declining price trend. If the indexed prices could be maintained, this would impart an inflationary bias to the system.

The UNCTAD integrated program includes proposals to encourage processing of raw materials in the commodity-exporting countries. Here the LDCs' desire for higher revenues from raw material exports is reinforced by the longer-run goals of industrialization and export diversification. Northern nations typically levy a low tariff on unprocessed primary products and successively higher rates on more processed forms. The effect of this "tariff escalation" is to discourage processing in the exporting countries, and the developing nations have emphasized the role of tariff escalation in accounting for the small fraction of total processing now performed in LDCs.

Since world efficiency would be increased by allowing processing to take place where real costs are lowest, the processing proposal is potentially an important one. However, a number of producing nations already apply countervailing policies such as export taxes or quotas on unprocessed raw materials, so that it is not obvious that elimination of the relevant Northern trade barriers would, by itself, have a major effect. Other considerations influencing the location of processing facilities include scale economies, tax policy, and political climate. In any case, the gains to LDCs from expanded processing will occur only over time and after substantial required investments have been made. Furthermore, for the Northern importing nations, who now account for the lion's share of all processing, elimination of cascaded tariffs could mean more rapid growth of competing imports from LDCs, exacerbating the already troublesome problem of internal adjustment for these nations.

FOUR

Toward a Preferred Regime

There is now widespread agreement concerning the desirability of a more equal distribution of world wealth between North and South but far less agreement concerning the appropriate means by which this objective can be achieved. In assessing the alternatives, it is essential to recognize that we live in an imperfect world. On the one hand, pervasive inefficiency or "slack" in the economic system implies that appropriately chosen policies could produce gains to all parties or at least to some without corresponding losses to others. On the other hand, political and institutional constraints often rule out the use of policies that promote overall economic efficiency. Thus, while redistribution of world income through commodity trade is acknowledged to be an imperfect and inefficient means of achieving redistribution, it must be compared with real alternatives, not with hypothetically efficient ones.

The analysis in the foregoing sections leads us to conclude that both North and South have much to gain from cooperative action in primary-commodity trade. The LDCs cannot unilaterally impose a new economic order upon the nations of the North; to achieve a substantial increase in Southern wealth and economic power, the active cooperation of the North is required. And it may well be in the North's own narrowly defined interest to provide this cooperation, for without it the South has little stake in maintaining a "moderate" world order.

The leverage commanded by Southern nations through their

control over key natural resources can be better employed as a tool in negotiation than as a weapon in confrontation. Unilateral action by producers is likely to be short-lived in its effectiveness. While the South is surely capable of inflicting substantial short-run damage upon the North, the very use of this option diminishes its effectiveness. The rich nations of the North can respond in the short run with confrontation tactics of their own and in the long run by insulating themselves from the power of LDC commodity producers. Closure is a costly choice for the North, but it could be fatal to the economic prospects of the South. Redistribution between rich and poor is far more feasible within the context of an open and rapidly growing world economy.

The increasing strength and awareness of Southern commodity exporters have made unilateral control by Northern consumers increasingly difficult. While the North can in the long run achieve virtually any desired degree of protection from the South's commodity weapon, the cost of doing so would be immense. Furthermore, closure by the North would entail foregoing the substantial gains from trade with an increasingly prosperous South. The North's security of supply can be greatly enhanced through a moderate international order that presents to the South a real possibility of gains without resort to confrontation.

Despite the considerable gains to be achieved through North-South cooperation in the primary-commodity area, past and present international commodity agreements have not been structured in such a way as to achieve these gains. On the other hand, it should be emphasized that a laissez faire policy is unlikely to produce competitive conditions in the markets for most key primary commodities. The inherent structure of production and consumption in these markets makes a unilateral control regime, possibly unstable in character, a far more probable outcome. Thus, a decision to refrain from explicit official action governing trade in commodities cannot be justified on the basis of theoretical benefits of perfectly competitive markets. Rather, laissez faire must be assessed in terms of the virtues and defects of the oligopolistic structures that are more likely to emerge under these circumstances.

On the basis of our analysis of the four basic types of commodity market organization, we have identified elements of a preferred commodity regime—one that achieves to some degree the underlying objectives of redistribution, stability, and security and that is likely to move commodity trade in the direction of greater rather than less overall economic efficiency. Although increased overall efficiency is not currently a high priority for negotiators on either side, we believe that the long-term interests of nations in both groups depend crucially upon maintaining a high rate of growth in the world economy.

We have divided the elements of our preferred regime into two groups. The first group contains those changes that appear to be workable within the current complex of political and institutional constraints. The second group includes changes that are in basic conflict with current political and institutional arrangements but could perhaps be achieved after a period of evolution of the international order.

CHANGES WITHIN THE CURRENT SYSTEM

These proposed changes achieve varying degrees of stability, security, redistribution, and increased efficiency while requiring a minimum degree of basic structural change in the current economic order. The measures are arranged below in order of increasing required adjustment. In making our recommendations, we recognize that commodity markets may differ significantly in their underlying structures. For this reason, we do not endorse a "unified approach" that applies the same international arrangements to all or most commodities. Our list of recommended measures does not include the establishment of international buffer stocks for a broad range of commodities.[24] We believe that such arrangements would be costly and prone to continuing conflict concerning appropriate floor and ceiling prices, intervention rules, and sources of funding. Instead, we advocate a

[24]Producers and/or consumers would still be able to set up their own buffering facilities for individual commodities, as in the past. However, we do not endorse the establishment of buffer stocks on a general basis or the provision of required financing by an international organization such as UNCTAD.

two-pronged approach to the problem of fluctuating prices: export-earnings stabilization and reinforced price stabilization through market transactions.

Export-Earnings Stabilization

As we have emphasized above, the objective of protecting LDC commodity exporters from short-term fluctuations in export earnings can be achieved without direct intervention in commodity markets. This protection can be provided even when measures to stabilize price around its long-term trend are unsuccessful or in the face of an unanticipated change in that trend. In light of the poor record of previous official price stabilization efforts, a separate earnings stabilization plan would be desirable even if official buffer stocks are maintained.

The International Monetary Fund already has an export-earnings-stabilization facility in operation. While it seems reasonable to build upon that facility, we would recommend several changes from current IMF practice. We advocate a shift from the overall balance-of-payments disequilibrium approach to an "insurance" basis, allowing commodity-by-commodity earnings stabilization. To separate aid from stabilization, interest charges should be at a market rate, with subsidies available for the poorest nations.

Strengthening Private Market Stabilization

Although private market transactions are motivated by the quest for profits rather than for stability, there is considerable theoretical and practical evidence that market transactions constitute an important stabilizing force. We recognize that speculative transactions can sometimes amplify price movements resulting from changes in underlying market conditions, but that official intervention in commodity markets by national governments or international agencies is also likely to provide incentives for destabilizing speculation. We believe that the prospects for effective direct official action to improve price stability at an acceptable cost are poor and that official action may in some cases prove disruptive. Our preferred approach is to reinforce the scope of market transactions that promote price stability and allow producers and consumers to protect themselves from future price movements through contractual arrangements.

Private futures markets already allow producers and consumers to buy some protection from future price movements. However, it would be desirable to encourage more complete and longer-term contractual arrangements than are now available. Improved international enforcement of futures contracts would be an important step in this direction. Such action could be undertaken through the General Agreement on Tariffs and Trade (GATT). Also, since erratic intervention in commodity markets by national governments is currently an important factor in depressing private stabilization activities, international agreements limiting actions such as price controls and export restraints could promote stability and security.

Elimination of Trade Barriers

The industrialized nations have already eliminated most tariff and quota restrictions on noncompeting imports, such as tropical products. However, for commodities also produced at home, import restrictions still protect politically powerful domestic producers and also often discriminate among LDC producers of competing imports. (The case of sugar is perhaps the most egregious example.) These trade barriers should be phased out and access to industrialized markets placed on an equal basis for all foreign suppliers. By doing this, the industrialized nations can improve overall world economic efficiency while eliminating costly distortions within their own economies. Furthermore, a unilateral step in this direction will lend much needed credibility to the North's rhetorical free market stance on the commodity issue.

Expansion of Processing

Most industrialized nations levy progressively higher tariffs on more processed forms of primary commodities, and these "cascaded'' tariff structures are one factor currently impeding the growth of processing activities within less-developed commodity-exporting nations.[25] Because other considerations play a major role in determining the location of processing activities, phasing out of these barriers could only facilitate, not ensure, a major shift in location. Nevertheless, this is another step that could be taken unilaterally by the North, yielding long-run efficiency gains to themselves as well as to Southern nations.

Expansion of processing in LDCs would require substantial capital investments. While private sources might generate some of the necessary funds, a special loan facility within the World Bank to channel capital for this purpose might also be desirable. However, interest rates on such project loans should be at market rates to guarantee that processing facilities are established only in those industries and countries likely to be competitive without prolonged special or differential treatment.

FUNDAMENTAL CHANGES

While implementation of the measures discussed above would require some potentially disruptive internal adjustments, the proposed changes are nonetheless broadly consistent with current international relationships. Below we discuss two additional proposals that depart in significant ways from basic features of the current system. Both proposals would require a substantial sacrifice of national sovereignty and are thus less viable for the immediate future than those discussed above. However, these proposals deserve serious consideration, particularly in long-term perspective, since they entail important potential benefits for both North and South. The first proposal would facilitate an immediate expansion of income redistribution between rich and poor nations; the second would enhance the long-run prospects of the LDCs by strengthening overall market efficiency and thus promoting rapid growth of the world economy.

[25]As previously noted, some LDCs already have countervailing incentives.

Commodity Tax Transfers

The principle of taxation to finance intra-nation redistribution is well established. Although it falls far short of the economist's ideal of a tax that does not distort economic incentives, the progressive income tax is generally viewed as the best available means of financing redistributive transfers within nations. However, little success has been achieved in extending this principle to international redistribution. United Nations designation of official development assistance targets, most recently 0.7 percent of GNP, has not prevented a continuing decline in the actual proportion. For a number of years, alternative transfer channels have been debated. Among these, the most prominent have been the Special Drawing Right (SDR) link proposal, which would have used the seigniorage from creation of special drawing rights by the IMF and, more recently, the earmarking of revenues from seabed mineral exploitation.

We propose a moderate international tax levied on all primary-commodity trade as another potential (alternative or supplementary) transfer channel that could be used to engineer a sizable redistribution of income from richer to poorer nations. As noted earlier, such a tax would raise prices paid by consumers while lowering those received by producers. Taxes collected could be rebated in full to most LDC producers and consumers. (A per capita income criterion would exclude most oil-exporting countries from the rebates.) The remainder of the revenue would be available to finance additional grant or soft loan aid to the poorest nations. Thus, the overall program could have a marked redistributive impact. Given the difficulties inherent in other methods of raising funds for redistributive transfers, any mild inefficiencies resulting from this plan[26] are likely to be outweighed by its benefits. Certainly the use of this moderate, broad-based price-raising scheme would be preferable in both efficiency and distributive impact to plans dependent upon larger increases in the prices of just a few commodities.

---

[26]As noted earlier, if private discount rates exceed appropriate social rates, a reduced level of production and consumption may increase overall efficiency.

An obvious alternative to the commodity trade tax is a tax on all international trade. However, there are two considerations that favor restricting the base to commodities. First, because supply and demand for primary commodities are relatively inelastic, the resulting allocational distortions would be smaller. Second, the commodity tax would impede neither Southern imports of capital goods required for industrialization nor Southern exports of industrial products. A further impetus to industrialization would be achieved if taxes rebated to exporting nations were *not* passed on to producers.

Calculations based on Table 1 indicate that a 5 percent tax on all international primary-commodity trade would have generated revenue of approximately $10 billion in 1973. Of this, about $2 billion would have been required to make full rebates to all non-OPEC LDC exporters, and perhaps another $1 billion would have been needed to eliminate the burden of higher prices on non-OPEC LDC consumers.[27] Thus, about $7 billion of the total revenue would have been available to finance additional redistributive transfers. This amount is equal to around 60 percent of *all* North-South redistributive transfers in the same year.[28]

We do not wish to minimize the difficulties inherent in this tax-transfer proposal. Obviously, whatever political problems complicate the allocation of other multilateral foreign aid flows would be present in this program as well. Furthermore, the incidence of the tax among the industrialized nations has no particular claim to equity. Since the tax would produce a net terms-of-trade deterioration for both producers and consumers, the largest bur-

[27]These rough calculations were made on the assumption of unchanged trade flows. In fact, total trade would be reduced by the tax. The amount of the reduction in trade and, hence, in revenue generated would depend on supply and demand elasticities for the various commodities and on the extent to which tax rebates were passed along to producers and consumers.

[28]This comparison is based upon total net official development assistance (ODA) and other official flows from Development Assistance Committee countries to developing nations and multilateral agencies. The total for 1973 was $11.8 billion, which includes both grants and concessional loans. Strictly speaking, the comparison should include only the grant component. See "Organisation for Economic Co-operation and Development," *Development Co-operation: 1977 Review*, OECD, Paris, 1977, pp. 165–166.

dens relative to GNP would fall upon those nations, such as Japan and Australia, that are major importers or exporters. For this reason, the commodity tax scheme might best be used to supplement other international types of revenue-producing arrangements. Finally, deliberate enactment of a new trade tax is in conflict with the rhetoric (although perhaps not the reality) of present multilateral negotiations to reduce barriers to trade.

International Trading Rules

We have already indicated that laissez faire policies in no way ensure competitive outcomes in international trade. However, new trading rules governing the actions of both producer and consumer nations could strengthen competitive forces in primary-commodity markets. Although oligopolistic elements could not be eliminated entirely, effective enforcement of rules restricting collusive behavior by producers or consumers could greatly increase the competitiveness of most markets. Market performance could also be improved through international enforcement of the provisions of voluntary long-term producer-consumer contracts.

Unfortunately, the obstacles to early action along these lines are formidable. Given the atmosphere of suspicion and antagonism that now pervades North-South economic and political relations, few countries of either group would currently support the required institutional changes. Commodity-exporting nations that now look to producers' organizations as a means of achieving a substantial earnings increase are unlikely to abjure this potentially powerful tool. Likewise, industrial consumers will surely distrust any international agreement that restricts their freedom of action, particularly when the international enforcement agency may be dominated by the LDC bloc. Thus, the required sacrifices of national sovereignty will not be immediately forthcoming. But successful North-South cooperation along some of the other lines discussed above could pave the way for progress in this area also.

An Oceans Regime for the 1980s

Ann L. Hollick

ONE

The Evolving Oceans Regime

INTRODUCTION

Because of the rapid improvement in technologies to exploit marine resources, the twentieth century is witnessing a radical change in the regime for the oceans. At the beginning of the century, the oceans could be characterized economically as a common property resource and, politically and socially, as a global commons. This situation in which ocean resources exceeded our capabilities to utilize them has now changed, and a number of marine resources have become scarce. As early as the middle of this century, some fisheries and whale species were already being overfished. The growth of shipping traffic has posed the problem of crowding and the danger of collision in certain re-stricted sea areas. And in the near-shore waters of Europe and Japan, the ocean's capacity to absorb pollutants from the land and from ships has been exceeded.

As oceanic resources have gained a scarcity value, the gov-ernments of the world have tried in various ways to lay claim to these resources, that is, to appropriate portions of the global commons. The predominant means of subjecting ocean resources to national control has been through the extension of coastal-state jurisdiction to ever-larger offshore areas. In 1930, the Hague Conference on the Progressive Codification of International Law considered a possible treaty providing for a 3-mile territorial sea. In subsequent years the legal concept of the "contiguous zone" was developed and, at the 1958 United Nations Conference on the Law of the Sea (UNCLOS), the concept was formulated to apply coastal-state fiscal, sanitation, and customs jurisdiction to a distance of 12 miles. The same Conference also approved a new means of measuring offshore zones—from straight baselines no longer than 24 miles drawn from headland to headland rather than from the coastline itself. A further national appropriation of coastal resources was recognized in the 1958 Convention on the Continental Shelf, which granted coastal states "sovereign rights" to seabed resources out to depths of 200 meters or, beyond that point, to water depths at which exploitation is possible. The underlying cause of these extensions of coastal-state jurisdiction is captured in the notion of the "exploitability clause" of the Convention on the Continental Shelf. As the technological capability evolved to exploit resources of the formerly inaccessible portions of oceans, coastal states were quick to appropriate those areas. Indeed, coastal-state claims soon began to outpace technological capability, commercial feasibility, or even concrete evidence of resource availability.

The trend of the past 50 years to enclose new ocean areas within national jurisdiction can be expected to continue and, indeed, to intensify during the final quarter of this century. The consequences of these developments for the 1980s are discussed below. This trend is contrasted with a "preferred" oceans regime that would partially reverse the movement toward national appropriations of ocean space. A preferred regime would adopt management policies designed to maximize material well-being, to satisfy national concerns with dignity, and to promote certainty in the use of the oceans.

THE THIRD UNITED NATIONS CONFERENCE ON THE LAW OF THE SEA

The appropriation by coastal and island states of vast areas of ocean space is a salient fact of the third quarter of the twentieth century and of the UN conferences that have addressed oceans issues in 1958, 1960, and since 1973. The prospect now exists of national appropriation of all ocean space in the final quarter of the century. At the Third United Nations Conference on the Law of the Sea (UNCLOS III),[1] national claims to 200-mile economic zones have received considerable acceptance. In addition, serious consideration is being given to recognition of coastal-state jurisdiction over the continental margin where it extends beyond 200 miles. Further vast areas of the oceans are being appropriated to national control by the use of the archipelago concept. This novel legal precept would link widely separated islands by straight lines. The enclosed waters would become "archipelagic waters" and would belong to the island nations, as would the 200-mile economic zones extending outward from the enclosing lines. Although these various claims appropriate over 40 percent of ocean space, there is no reason to think coastal nations will stop here. Indeed, the evidence is abundant that a number of states bordering on the vast oceans are considering national claims to resources "adjacent to" their 200-mile zones even when there is no continental margin beyond that distance.

Other features of UNCLOS III merit detailed consideration since they, too, set the stage for the oceans regime of the 1980s. The most obvious fact of the present Conference is that it is a political, not a technical or management, undertaking. What is being attempted at UNCLOS III is the formulation of a compromise treaty that will satisfy the perceived interests of a majority of the 148 participating nations across a wide range of issues. Since the agenda is impossibly long (25 items and over 100 subitems) and the perceived vital interests of many of the participants are in direct conflict on many issues, the outcome of the Conference is uncertain. Whether or not a treaty is voted, signed, and ratified, the Conference has produced negotiating texts as well as a legislative history that delineate general rules and new jurisdictional rights that can set the broad outlines of a future regime. Even if the Conference participants should fail to reach agreement, many states will proceed to promulgate those

[1]The Third United Nations Conference on the Law of the Sea began officially in December 1973. It was preceded by three years of preparatory work.

rules and jurisdictional claims that suit their particular situation. Among the new legal concepts that have developed to satisfy various national aspirations are those of archipelagic waters and "archipelagic sea-lanes," "exclusive economic zones," and the right of transit through international straits. These formulations, as elaborated in the negotiating text, represent efforts to compromise and balance an expanded coastal-state jurisdiction with international interests in the newly claimed areas. Given the preponderant number of coastal states, 82 by their own reckoning, it is not surprising that the balance leans toward coastal states rather than toward international rights. Where a compromise has been difficult to achieve, the drafters have resorted to ambiguous language that may allow both sides to support the treaty now but that will be the subject of conflicting interpretations in the future.

An issue directly linked to planned offshore claims and yet politically intractable within a general law of the sea agreement is that of boundaries—both between adjacent and opposite states and between national and international areas. Boundaries based on underwater topography do not necessarily coincide with median or equidistant lines drawn from the coastline. They will ultimately have to be negotiated on a case-by-case basis or resolved by force.

The judicial settlement procedures presently under review at the Conference will contribute little to the settlement of boundary or other disputes unless all parties to a particular dispute agree to submit their differences to a single, binding form of dispute settlement. The draft text suggests that parties to the treaty may choose among several dispute-settlement procedures (e.g., arbitration, a Law of the Sea Tribunal, the International Court of Justice). It also lists a number of areas that will be limited to conciliation or excluded from dispute-settlement altogether. They include (1) the delimitation of boundaries, (2) matters pertaining to the coastal state's rights to control fishing or marine scientific research in its exclusive economic zone, and (3) military activities. Clearly these are among the most controversial issues and therefore the most deserving of compulsory and binding dispute settlement.

The Conference is also considering the establishment of an international authority to regulate exploitation of deep-sea nodules and an international "enterprise" to mine nodules directly. At the present level of knowledge and technology, nodules containing manganese, nickel, copper, and cobalt will be the only resource of consequence left beyond nationally claimed areas of jurisdiction. It remains to be seen whether the value of this resource will finance the elaborate international machinery that some developing countries hope to build. Apart from the doubtful prospect for substantial revenues from deep-sea mining, prospects for an international mining authority are further dimmed by the likelihood that the technologically advanced countries in association with some developing nations will begin to mine the nodules without waiting for agreement on an international regime. A further problem for a deep-sea mining regime lies in the as yet unarticulated plans of some Pacific Ocean coastal and island nations to extend their jurisdiction to embrace some of the more attractive nodule sites.

Given the irreconcilable and strongly held positions represented in the present Law of the Sea debates, it seems a foregone conclusion that the Conference will not resolve outstanding ocean issues. Any treaty that it might adopt would necessarily have to skirt the more intractable problems, leaving them to the 1980s and beyond. What is a matter for greater concern is whether the outcome of the Conference will exacerbate the problems that must ultimately be resolved if the oceans are to be managed properly.[2]

[2]In seeking agreement, for instance, the direction of the Conference has been toward acquiescence in the maximum demands of coastal states—a trend that may prove difficult to rectify when the difficulties inherent in such an approach start to mount.

TWO

A Prospective Oceans Regime for the 1980s

On the basis of developments at UNCLOS III as well as of trends in marine-resource use, one can draw a rough sketch of the probable oceans regime of the 1980s. In brief, it is evident that ocean-resource exploitation will continue to increase, as will the problems of crowding and "negative externalities," such as ocean pollution and overfishing. The bulk of ocean-resource activities will be carried on within 200-mile zones under the regulation and control of national governments. Conflicts will arise over the delineation of national boundaries as well as over the interaction of national and international uses of the zone and their impact on neighboring states. Mining of manganese nodules will begin in the Pacific Ocean, either under the auspices of an international regulatory authority or through private and state organizations operating without reference to an international organization.

JURISDICTIONAL DISPUTES

Contention over the substance and the scope of coastal-state jurisdiction in the oceans will be a salient feature of the 1980s oceans regime. Substantive conflicts may take a number of forms. Traditional high-seas freedoms, such as navigation or the laying of pipelines and cables, will have to be reconciled with the coastal states' new authority over zones of 200 miles or more. Other conflicts may arise among and between neighboring coastal states where activities within a nation's offshore zones, such as the dumping or discharge of wastes, have adverse consequences for nearby states.

The determination of the physical extent of a coastal state's jurisdiction in accordance with the conflicting norms that have been advocated at UNCLOS III will be problematic. States that are situated opposite or adjacent to one another will have to resolve their boundary differences by negotiation or force where the equidistance or median-line principle applicable to the waters does not coincide with the depth contours of a shared continental-shelf area. The problems of this nature between the United States and Canada are minor compared with those in the South China Sea, East China Sea, or the Aegean, where a multiplicity of states and significant historical and political animosities further complicate the difficulties posed by geography. Islands of disputed ownership create particular problems, and it is possible that these disputes will take a violent direction where valuable offshore resources are involved. Uninhabited rocks and even submerged coral atolls are accepted in the Conference negotiating text as points from which national jurisdiction might be measured. Scrambles to acquire and control such economically attractive pieces of real estate will doubtless enliven the 1980s oceans scene.

Where states front on the major oceans, it is likely that, with or without a treaty, justifications will be found for the extension of coastal-state control beyond 200 miles even where there is no continental margin. Peru has already indicated its interest in the migratory fisheries beyond 200 miles, while Mexico is eyeing the prospect of nodule mining in the North Pacific beyond 200 miles. Opposition to the forces behind further national extensions will be weak. The landlocked and "geographically disadvantaged" states have had limited success in exerting their influence at UNCLOS III. And most of the maritime states, such as the United States, have substantial coastal interests that preclude wholehearted opposition to extension. The generous formulas that are now being considered for delimiting the extent of coastal-state jurisdiction over the continental margin suggest that expansionist forces will prevail in the 1980s and further reduce the size of the "common heritage of mankind."

PROBLEMS WITHIN THE 200-MILE ZONE

Although nationalist sentiments will continue to stimulate claims beyond 200 miles, exploration and exploitation of the resources of the economic zone will absorb most national energies in the 1980s. All the world's coastal fisheries and up to 95 percent of the offshore oil are found in this area.[3]

Fishing

The fishing activities of coastal states in the 1980s will vary from country to country and region to region. The direction of customary law as well as the Law of the Sea negotiating text is toward the phasing out of most distant-water fishing activities in favor of coastal-state fishing. Theoretically, according to the provisions of the present draft treaty, the coastal state should allow other nations to harvest that portion of the fishery (up to the level of maximum sustainable yield) that it cannot harvest itself. In practice, there are only limited conciliation provisions for contesting coastal-state actions under the proposed treaty if a state decides to prohibit all foreign fishing or, at the other extreme, to license foreign fishing in excess of what coastal fish stocks can bear. These decisions will be a matter of domestic politics, where short-term considerations can be expected to prevail. In the absence of countervailing forces, a particular government may allow excessive fishing for the sake of its immediate revenue needs. On the other hand, nationalist sentiments spurred by domestic fishing interests may urge a ban on all foreign fishing to reduce the local industry's own costs of operation regardless of the fishery resource that may go underutilized. In the absence of effective governmental management restricting entry into the coastal fishery, the domestic fishing industries are likely to become overcapitalized and, ultimately, to overfish the national zones. Although the situation will vary from country to country and from government to government, the general trend will be toward the replacement of long-distance fishing fleets and factory

[3]National Petroleum Council, *Ocean Petroleum Resources,* report, Washington, D.C., March 1975.

ships with possibly less efficient coastal fishing and shore-based processing operations.

Even where a government chooses to manage a coastal fishery to achieve a maximum or an optimum yield, its efforts may be undermined by the activities of neighboring states. This problem will be especially acute in enclosed areas, such as the Caribbean and the Mediterranean. In these seas, coastal stocks are so intermingled that management must be undertaken on a regional, not a national, basis. The distribution of the fishery resource simply does not coincide with artificial boundaries. It is likely, however, that the 1980s will see serious problems of overfishing before this lesson is learned and regional management practices are adopted. For countries such as the United States and Canada, these problems will not arise along the major expanses of coastline. At the borders with other countries, however, coordinated management will be needed.

Anadromous[4] and highly migratory species, salmon and tuna, respectively, pose a special set of problems that cannot be resolved by 200-mile resource zones. Salmon migrate to and from their spawning rivers in patterns that take them well beyond 200 miles from shore. Fishing beyond the 200-mile zone in the 1980s could be a major source of contention between Japan and the various host countries of the Northern Pacific. The direction this dispute takes will depend upon the overall condition of Japan's fishing industry and upon bilateral agreements that it is willing or forced to make with the United States, Canada, and the Soviet Union.

The management of tuna stocks will be even more difficult politically since it involves a larger number of states. Tuna travel at high speeds and migrate great distances around and across the Indian, Atlantic, and Pacific oceans. Management schemes must be applied to the stock as a whole, or the result could be overfishing and depletion of the resource. If each country were to fish tuna at will as schools passed within 200 miles of its shores, the fishery might become depleted. In the context of the Law

---

[4]Anadromous species spawn in fresh water but spend most of their lives at sea.

of the Sea Conference and its negotiating text, no concrete provisions have been made for this special problem. The prospect for the 1980s, therefore, is increased pressure on the tuna stocks and continued overcapacity within the distant-water tuna fleets.

As distant-water fleets are progressively squeezed out of national economic zones and pressures on migratory stocks increase, distant-water vessels are turning to the living resources of the Antarctic. The Japanese and Russians are already exploiting Antarctic krill. In the absence of a regime to limit access to this fishery, the resource may be severely reduced in the 1980s, with adverse effects on the whales that feed on krill. UNCLOS III has not addressed the issue of Antarctic resources, fisheries, or otherwise. The signatories of the 1959 Antarctic Treaty will continue to do so with uncertain results. In addition to the intrinsic difficulties of negotiating a limited access regime for any fishery, the Antarctic situation is complicated by the fact that Argentina, Australia, Chile, France, New Zealand, Norway, and the United Kingdom have all laid claim to sectors of the Antarctic and its waters.

Whether international management schemes are adopted in the 1980s for the Antarctic, for migratory species, for anadromous species, or for coastal stocks that move across national boundaries will depend upon new perceptions of interdependence in this area and of the need for this source of protein over the long run. The political will to forgo a degree of national sovereignty in fisheries management will probably be achieved only after depletion of stocks and a period of controversy over respective national management schemes.

Petroleum

Slightly over one-fifth of global petroleum production comes from the exploitation of offshore reserves. Most of this has been recovered close to shore at depths of less than 200 meters. Present estimates indicate that over two-thirds of the petroleum reserves of the continental margin may be beyond present territorial waters. Given the fact that petroleum will continue to supply the major portion of world energy needs through the 1980s, the oil and gas of the continental margin will be an important element in the world energy picture. Only 1 to 5 percent of world offshore oil and gas is estimated to lie on the margin beyond 200 miles. The combination of distance from shore and increasing depths as exploitation moves farther offshore will restrict commercial activities in the 1980s to areas within the economic zone. As oil exploitation moves to greater depths within the zone, surface rigs and platforms will be replaced by underwater mining and storage equipment. This will make them immune to most inclement weather, but, like surface operations, they can pose a hazard to navigation and will have to be well marked.

Assuming the resolution of differences over boundaries, the recovery of petroleum from the continental margin will not pose the same problem as fishing in national 200-mile zones. Unless an oil pool happens to cross an ocean boundary, cooperative management arrangements will not be necessary. Where the common-pool problem arises, bilateral or multilateral agreement will have to be reached if inefficient drilling into the shared pool is to be avoided. Cooperative arrangements may also prove desirable with regard to the storage of oil or its movement by pipeline or ship. Norwegian oil from the North Sea, for instance, is presently being brought ashore in Scotland.

With the increased exploitation of offshore reserves in the 1980s will come greater numbers of blowouts and accidental spills. Apart from general injunctions to prevent marine pollution, no specific regulations have been considered at the Law of the Sea Conference which would determine environmental standards for offshore-resource exploitation. Each nation will be free to specify its own antipollution regulations and may, in some instances, prefer to set minimal or no standards as an inducement to investment. The development of such "pollution havens" would create negative externalities for neighboring zones where environmental goals may be valued for aquaculture, aesthetics, tourism, or other purposes. Given the transnational impact of offshore pollution, the states of the region will have to band together in setting standards if environmental goals are to be pursued. Coercive measures may prove to be the only means to ensure that recalcitrant states observe similar antipollution measures in their respective zones.

Other Energy-related Uses

Negative externalities may arise from any of a number of energy-related uses a state chooses to make of its zone. In its quest for energy, the coastal state may be expected to turn to its offshore areas to site nuclear power plants, to capture tidal energy, to build vast kelp farms (bioconversion), or to harness solar energy (ocean thermal-energy conversion). The fears of a core meltdown in nuclear power plants are widespread, and offshore siting has become increasingly attractive where public opposition to onshore locations exists. Indeed, coastal states may respond to domestic pressures by locating plants as far from shore as possible—that is, at the edge of the 200-mile zone. (This might be especially the case where the energy generated supports offshore industrial activities that are not wanted near population centers.) Even in the absence of a power plant failure, the normal operation of a nuclear plant entails environmental change through the discharge of heated water. The attendant impact on the local fisheries population may represent a positive or a negative externality. (That is, raising the water temperature a few degrees may make the environment more or less congenial to fish stocks, depending on normal temperatures and on the types of stocks that might flourish in the warmed waters.) In any case, neighboring states will object to action over which they have no control and which poses potential environmental damage. The other nonconventional forms of energy from the oceans will still be in the experimental stage in the 1980s and hence will not represent a major source of friction in the use of economic zones.

Pollution

The pollution of the ocean by the dumping of waste materials offshore or by the direct emission of sewage into ocean or river waters has widespread as well as local effects. The use of the ocean as a disposal medium will increase in the 1980s with the growth of coastal populations and greater agricultural (pesticides) and industrial activities. The negative externalities of dumping and land-source pollution will depend upon (1) where the dumping takes place, (2) the proximity of other zones, (3) the depth of the ocean areas, and (4) the direction of winds and ocean currents. International incidents could arise over the dumping of wastes in areas that may be remote from the coastal state's local population but that would affect the population or marine resources of other coastal states.

COMMERCIAL NAVIGATION

The tonnage of the world merchant fleet has grown dramatically over the past 25 years. The size and speed of merchant ships have increased substantially.[5] These trends will continue throughout the 1980s despite fluctuations resulting from petroleum price increases and reduced energy demand. As the volume of merchant shipping has grown, the number of collisions and groundings has increased. Accidents have reached the point where, on average, a 50,000-ton ship sinks every day. Larger ships and greater numbers of them mean that ever more costly accidents will occur in the 1980s. The major shipping routes around the world are in the calmer waters within 200 miles of land. Shipping therefore will be competing for space with the increased resource exploitation that will be under way in the 200-mile zones.

Tanker collisions with unmarked installations can be averted by adopting prominent markings and by requiring coastal states to issue detailed and updated charts designating obstacles to navigation. Some states may object to any requirements that they facilitate international navigation in their economic zones and may not cooperate. Others may not have the technical ca-

[5]From a world fleet of 81.6 GRT (gross registered tons) in 1950, commercial shipping had increased to 342.2 GRT by 1975, according to *Lloyd's Register of Shipping*. Tanker size has increased from less than 50,000 dwt. (dead weight tons) to 325,000 dwt. in the space of a dozen years, with even larger vessels under construction. And containerships capable of 33 knots are setting new transoceanic speed records.

pability or financial resources to implement these measures regularly.

On the subject of navigation, the UNCLOS text will do little more than provide for the right of coastal states to establish traffic lanes in archipelagic waters and straits overlapped by 12-mile territorial seas. After a number of serious collisions and groundings, coastal states will be tempted to assert national control over the congested area. This could result in friction between the shippers and the coastal states. Alternatively, the recognition of a mutual interest in regulating traffic in congested areas may lead to international forms of regulation. States might, for example, turn to the Intergovernmental Maritime Consultative Organization (IMCO) in the 1980s with problems of navigation in congested areas.

DEEP-SEABED MINING

Mining of the deep-seabed manganese nodules in the 1980s will be in its early stages. It will be an expensive undertaking, and this expense plus the technological uncertainties and political controversies that may attend deep-sea mining will pose problems for the first generation of mining operations. Even if technical and political difficulties are ironed out, the availability of low-cost, land-based supplies of cobalt, manganese, nickel, and copper may slow the rate of growth of deep-sea mining during the last quarter of the century.

The legal arrangements that will govern deep-sea mining in the 1980s are difficult to predict at this time. UNCLOS III has, in the course of its deliberations, developed a broad consensus that the international seabed mining authority should include an assembly, a council, a secretariat, an operating body (the enterprise), regulatory commissions, and a tribunal. Certain central issues, however, continue to divide the industrialized and the developing states. Developed countries prefer a mining system in which private or state entities will be assured the right to mine the seabed under license by the international authority. The authority could also mine the seabed through an operating arm called the ''enterprise.'' The Group of 77, speaking for developing nations, has adopted the position that, after an initial period of 20 or so years, only the international seabed authority should be allowed to mine the deep seabed. If this cannot be agreed at a future review conference, then an automatic moratorium on further licensing of mine sites would come into effect. An accommodation between these two views has been difficult and the problems have been compounded by fissures within the ranks of the developing countries. If the industrialized and wealthiest developing states opt for undertaking their own mining operations and the nations of the Pacific attempt to carve out pieces of the ocean as prospective sites, there is little likelihood that mining in the 1980s will be regulated by an international organization. On the other hand, if an international institution is successfully negotiated, the limited revenues that will be generated from seabed mining in the 1980s and throughout the rest of the century will be consumed by the cost of the elaborate organization that is envisioned.

MILITARY USES

From a military perspective, the oceans are important in maintaining the strategic deterrent that makes a first-strike nuclear attack too costly. The opaque ocean environment offers a safe place for United States and Soviet ballistic submarines and thereby contributes to the maintenance of a fragile peace. Technological change has a major impact on the viability of a strategic balance as the superpowers continually seek means to detect enemy submarines while making their own ever more invulnerable. Competitive technological change in antisubmarine warfare (ASW) and in submarine construction will doubtless continue throughout the 1980s. While improvements in ASW technology may render the submarine more vulnerable, a countervailing factor making it more difficult to detect will be the increased background noise resulting from greater commercial use of the oceans. Commercial activities will provide new hiding places for, and help to mask the characteristic signature of, submarines.

No explicit restrictions on military activity per se have evolved

186

out of the Conference. This will create an interesting situation in the 1980s: the coastal state will be consolidating its control over the resources of its 200-mile zone while the same area may be used by other nations for strategic or tactical military purposes. The wealthier coastal states will develop the military forces to protect offshore operations such as oil rigs or fishing from sabotage or harassment. Some coastal states may acquiesce in the use of their zones as hiding places or sanctuaries for submarines and other warships of friendly nations. Others may try to monitor or prohibit all ingress by foreign military vessels and installation of ASW equipment. Even small coastal states determined to prevent unwanted activities in their zones may easily develop the means for raising the costs of foreign military operations. Relatively inexpensive heat-seeking or other guided missiles may be installed on patrol boats charged with guarding national economic zones. These can inflict substantial damage to expensive ships or equipment at minimal cost to the coastal state.

As noted above, the oceans regime of the 1980s will be characterized by numerous disagreements and conflicts. Coastal patrol fleets may find themselves involved in the controversies that will arise from conflicting or incompatible uses of neighboring or nearby coastal zones or from disputes over the determination of boundaries. Military forces may also be deployed to protect commercial activities beyond national zones, such as deep-sea mining or navigation. The jurisdictional approach adopted by the Law of the Sea negotiations and the inability to agree on strong provisions for the settlement of disputes will result in a high level of ocean conflict in the 1980s and the intermittent resort to military force.

THREE

A Preferred Oceans Regime

In considering what might constitute an ideal oceans regime, it is readily apparent that no single ideal regime is agreeable to all. It is far easier to determine and agree upon what is not ideal. The outcome of the present Conference, for instance, and the prospects it heralds for the 1980s can scarcely be viewed as ideal whether from the perspective of equity, conflict avoidance, or optimal resource management. Indeed, if it suggests anything, UNCLOS III demonstrates how *not* to manage a global commons.

The notion of a commons has been applied to the oceans in two different senses. Traditionally it has meant an area that could be appropriated by no one, in which the supply of the resource exceeded the demand or capability to appropriate it, and where laissez faire behavior was the norm. This *res nullius* concept of the oceans commons has been supplanted by the newer notion of a *res communis*, in which the oceans are treated as an international public good that must be managed cooperatively and for the general welfare. Does either version of global commons generate self-evident norms that provide the blueprint for an ideal oceans regime? Regrettably, neither does. The notion of an ideal regime remains as elusive as ever—and as dependent upon the goals and purposes of the observer.

Human goals can suggest any number or variety of preferred regimes. Indeed, the oceans as a focal point would be irrelevant to regimes that some consider ideal. Some might prefer to structure management regimes along functional lines, such as food or energy, taking into account the multiple uses of the oceans.

They might, for instance, wish to create a regime to maximize and allocate the production of protein in the world to alleviate malnutrition. In such a food regime, ocean fisheries would be one component to be coordinated with other parts of the regime. Under this functional approach, decisions as to the type of fishing to encourage would consider the use of fish meal as livestock feed or fertilizer, and the final determination would be made according to a mix that yielded the maximum amount of protein for human consumption. The proper management of such a regime might call for the participation of farmers, people engaged in fishing, nutritionists, Agency for International Development (AID) officials, and so on. Similarly, if one were to create an energy regime that would attempt to provide overall management of world energy resources, the decisions and decision makers would differ significantly from those of an oceans or a food regime.

Because an oceans regime is basically a spatial concept, it cuts through many issue areas. Besides food and energy, these include minerals, environment, transportation, science, technology transfer, trade and commodity arrangements, and military security. Thus, preferred management schemes depend upon the way one wishes to "slice" the issues and the goals one wishes to pursue. The extent to which the observer aggregates or disaggregates interrelated issues is also a matter of personal preference. A proponent of world government might at one extreme favor a single management regime, while an advocate of diversity and local initiative might prefer to handle each issue separately.

Governments have opted for a spatial oceans regime. Having put all oceans issues, however loosely related, into a single negotiating forum, they have then proceeded to divide ocean space into discrete pieces of real estate. Regrettably for their plans, these proposed arrangements run counter to the facts of physical interdependencies across ocean boundaries. Ocean winds and currents will not observe artificial boundaries, nor will the living resources of the sea. Mismanagement of fisheries or environmental damage in one nation's offshore areas will affect neighboring states' areas to varying degrees. Thus, as we have seen in the above overview of the 1980s, negative externalities, conflicts, and, ultimately, a few cooperative arrangements will be the probable result of a regime based on purely jurisdictional and spatial concepts.

The following discussion represents merely one of several conceivable views as to a preferred regime for the oceans. Several assumptions on which this view rests must be clarified at the outset. First, the fact is accepted that oceans issues have, over a period of years, been treated in a single negotiating forum. Although it might be preferable to disassemble oceans discussions either into discrete or into broader issue forums, it is unlikely that an "oceans" focus will disappear entirely.[6]

A second assumption is that the regime likely to evolve out of the current Conference will be unstable. This instability provides an opportunity for the evolution of a better, if not the best, oceans regime. Taking into account the underlying physical interdependencies in the oceans, it may yet be possible to create a regime that is not only stable but also meets certain broad goals.

The third assumption is that a desirable oceans regime and its various components must be consistent with three broad objectives. First, it must serve to promote overall material well-being over the long run. The more real wealth that is generated, the more there will be to distribute. Second, it must promote national or collective dignity or self-esteem. This is, to be sure, a subjective concept and one that is difficult to translate into policy programs. Nonetheless it is crucial. It goes to the root of oceans policy issues concerned with perceptions of equity, such as distribution of revenues, participation in decision making, weighted

[6]To avoid completely disaggregating oceans from other issues will require the blending of oceans with related regimes through dual or expanded areas of competence for government oceans specialists. At present, a number of decision makers focus exclusively on oceans questions. Henceforth it would be hoped that governments would pursue personnel policies according to which an oceans specialist, such as a fisheries manager, would have broadly defined responsibilities promoting other related regimes, such as one to increase world protein. In this fashion the discrete subsystems of an oceans regime might be linked to other relevant issue areas. A spatial approach to oceans questions might thereby be usefully combined with related goal-oriented regimes.

voting, and so on. Finally, a desirable oceans regime must provide predictability or certainty in the enjoyment of material well-being and the condition of self-respect. This notion of certainty encompasses protection from unwanted eventualities and unpleasant surprises resulting from negative externalities as well as from conflict situations. These three touchstones do not provide a detailed blueprint for building an oceans regime; indeed, at times, they may lead to conflicting prescriptions. They do, however, provide a useful reference point against which to judge alternative oceans regimes and their component parts.

Applying the criteria of material well-being, dignity, and certainty to the regime that will evolve in the 1980s (if present trends in UNCLOS III are realized) highlights the sources of instability therein. The probable oceans regime will not elicit optimal management of global marine resources—particularly in the area of fisheries, navigation, and environmental protection. Although total ocean resources will not be maximized, some nations will benefit substantially from exclusive control of vast ocean areas. These nations, however, include among their number those that are the wealthiest. In fact, roughly half of the ocean space to be enclosed within 200-mile zones will go to developed countries.[7] Thus, in terms of promoting perceptions of equity and national dignity, the Conference must also fail. Among the 148 nations participating, approximately one-third will be excluded from the major benefits of the new regime because they lack coastlines or sizable offshore areas.

The issue of national self-respect is a particularly troublesome one in the context of the negotiations concerning an international mining authority. In fact, an international regime that promotes wide international participation in, and complete control of, seabed mining may be antithetical to a mining system that would be economically optimal. For instance, a mining authority including all UN members and based on a "one-nation one-vote" decision-making structure might prove a poor management body,

---

[7]Coastal states with continental margins that extend beyond 200 miles include Australia, Canada, Indonesia, the United States, the Soviet Union, New Zealand, and Argentina in descending order of area.

particularly if political considerations came to dominate its decisions. The sacrifice of one value in favor of the other must ultimately be squarely faced.

In terms of the third touchstone, that of security from unwelcome surprises, the prospective oceans regime of the 1980s fails most conspicuously. As noted earlier, the coastal-state and international rights being negotiated in UNCLOS III will be subject to dispute whether or not international agreement is reached. Even without a treaty, the legislative history of the Conference will become the basis for changes in regime. Differences of view (whether over boundaries, exclusion from fishing grounds, scientific research, navigation, etc.) will hamper the effective exploitation of resources, disrupt development plans, and provoke conflict. Additionally, activities in neighboring economic zones may generate negative externalities with the same disruptive consequences. In sum, the oceans regime evolving out of the Conference fails to optimize overall material well-being through wise management. Moreover, its distributional effect of making the rich richer runs counter to most perceptions of equity. The perception of inequity on the part of the poorer nations together with the management difficulties posed by a purely jurisdictional division of the oceans will generate conflict and uncertainty.

An oceans regime that promotes material well-being, dignity, and certainty could take a number of forms. However, it would fall within certain broad outlines. In the first place, it would not be based on carving the oceans into national zones of varying size. Such an approach fails to promote any of the three desiderata. A preferable regime would begin with the assumption that the oceans beyond a limited distance (such as 3 or 12 miles or 200 meters depth) are in fact owned by the international community rather than by individual coastal states. Within this international area, marine resources should be managed to optimize their production, and the revenues generated by their exploitation should be used to advance our scientific knowledge of the oceans and for other internationally agreed-upon purposes.

The maximization of revenues from ocean resources implies efficient use of the factors of production and will yield greater material benefits on a global scale. In delineating an oceans regime based on international management, it is easier to outline an approach that maximizes material well-being than it is to determine mechanisms for promoting equity, dignity, and self-respect. To facilitate this task, it is useful to distinguish between four distinct components of resource use: the product itself, the process of exploitation, the revenues that are generated by the recovery of the resource, and decision making with respect to all these aspects of resource use.

How optimal management is achieved will vary from resource to resource. *Fisheries*, for example, should be managed on the basis of ecological interdependence. From a biological perspective, access to the resource must be restricted to a level of fishing consistent with the stock's capacity to reproduce. From an economic perspective, efforts must be made to avoid overcapitalizing the fishery industry. To restrict access and to recover revenues from the resource, either an auction system or an appropriate tax must be applied. Decisions with regard to these and other management questions should be made by international commissions organized along regional lines. A form of weighted voting may be adopted within these commissions, where necessary, to take into account the political sensibilities of coastal states. The work of these commissions might be coordinated by a Food and Agriculture Organization (FAO) with improved regulatory powers. A competitive international market would be the most efficient means of allocating the fish catch. However, the revenues generated by auctioning or taxing access to the resource should be used to meet the protein requirements of the most needy states after deductions have been made to cover the costs of operating the fisheries commissions and of conducting the scientific research on whose information decisions of the commissions would be based. Such a fisheries regime could optimize revenues from the fisheries resource.[8] Because the regime would be conducted according to sound ecological principles and supported by on-

[8]Social and political considerations within certain countries might suggest that, at least for a transitional period, coastal fishing communities should be allowed to pursue their traditional methods of fishing and marketing.

going scientific information, it would provide a measure of pre-dictability not presently enjoyed in ocean fishing.

A regime conducive to the optimal exploitation of *petroleum or seabed minerals* might be constructed along different lines. Unlike fisheries, the process of exploitation of these resources does not necessarily create externalities for other users. That, of course, is not the case where oil pollution results from ex-ploitation or transport of the resource. In general, however, the absence of externalities means that oil exploitation can be man-aged efficiently on national or international lines. International regulations would be in order with respect to antipollution safe-guards or related areas of transport where externalities might exist. As to whether petroleum exploitation should be managed nationally or internationally, the weight of historical develop-ments is toward national management. While distant-water fleets have fished just beyond the territorial waters of coastal states, the practice with regard to petroleum has been toward coastal-state claims that exclude uninvited foreign activity. The 1958 Convention on the Continental Shelf reinforced the coastal-state claim when it provided for coastal-state sovereign rights over seabed resources to the depth of 200 meters or, beyond that point, to where the depth allowed exploitation.

By explicitly distinguishing between the product, the process of exploitation, the revenues generated, and the process of de-cision making, it might be possible to create a regime that coun-terbalances the weight of historical coastal-state claims with some recognition of international interests in seabed areas that have been regarded as non-national throughout most of human history. Optimal management of petroleum exploitation may in-deed be possible under national management that extends out-ward as technology allows and as coastal-state interests deter-mine. The resource will certainly not be wasted, as in the case of fisheries, if a state delays in recovering its offshore reserves. An absolute limit to coastal-state control of petroleum exploi-tation should, however, be set to prevent the appropriation of even greater seabed areas. That might be at any distance from shore. A limit of 200 miles would ensure that all probable ocean oil production would be under national management. (By the time it is commercially feasible to operate at the depths and distances beyond 200 miles from shore, the costs of alternative energy sources should make such remote offshore petroleum unattractive.) Such a limit therefore would not mitigate the inequity of dividing the petroleum resources of the oceans among a few coastal states with resource-rich continental margins. This might be accomplished by an international tax levied on the resources deriving from oil production beyond a limited coastal area—possibly 200 meters deep. This tax could be used for scientific research on oil pollution and alternative ways of coping with it, or it could be used to assist developing countries in meeting their energy needs. In particular, the revenues might be channeled into studies concerning the offshore siting of nuclear power plants and into the financing of energy-related technology transfer. Equity/dignity goals would be promoted by such revenue sharing as well as by international participation in decision making regarding siting, maintenance of shipping lanes, size of safety zones, marking of oil-related installations, and protection of the environment from marine pollution. The Intergovernmental Maritime Consultative Organization is the forum in which these kinds of decisions should be made.

Pollution is an externality that cuts across a number of ocean uses, whether they be navigation, fishing, or minerals exploitation. It consists of deliberate or accidental environmental alterations. The deliberate use of the oceans for the disposal of wastes via offshore dumping or discharges (through rivers or directly into the oceans) reflects another resource aspect of the oceans— the oceans as a repository for waste materials. The oceans have performed this function for centuries and may continue to do so for the indefinite future. Pending conclusive information on the local or global assimilative limits of the oceans, the use of the oceans for waste disposal should reflect the externalities thereby imposed on other users. Where dumping entails costs for a fishery, a kelp farm, an offshore power plant, or whatever, the polluter must be regarded as one of several competing users. As such, he or she must be willing to pay for the use of a disposal area. If it is worth more as something other than a dumping ground, other users would outbid the polluter, who would have to select an alternative, less expensive site. This or a similar principle must be applicable across as well as within national ocean boundaries. Where appropriate regional fisheries regulatory groups do exist, the negotiation for the use of ocean space must take place with the international fisheries commission concerned. Similarly, as international functional organizations evolve to handle other ocean uses, they, too, would be in a position to bid on alternative uses of ocean space. The revenues derived from such competitive bidding among ocean users might be directed to scientific studies of local and overall environmental conditions to improve the state of knowledge of the ocean environment. Security from environmental catastrophes would be the desired consequence.

As with fishing and waste disposal, *shipping* represents a time-honored use of the oceans. In the past two decades, the number of merchant ships has doubled and the tonnage has quadrupled. Given present rates of growth and the consequent externalities of congestion, ocean shipping must increasingly be subject to international management and regulation. Where ocean shipping does not create problems of congestion or generate externalities for other uses, as in the open ocean, the traditional laissez faire regime represents an optimal management approach to navigation. Environmental and other standards, of course, might constitute a possible exception to this laissez faire regime even in the open ocean. In intensively used near-shore areas, physical crowding may preclude simultaneous use by shippers and other users. In these instances, the determination of the use to be made of the area should, as in the case of dumping, be determined by a system that leads to the use with the highest economic value—possibly determined by competitive bidding. In areas where shipping congestion is the problem, such as at the entrances to ports and harbors or in straits such as Dover, Gibraltar, and Malacca, even improved navigational rules of the road will soon be inadequate to avoid groundings and collisions. Traffic will have to be managed, much as it presently is in airports, preferably by international bodies composed of the users and the nearby coastal states. To finance the costs of navigational aids and traffic control, user fees might be charged. These fees can also be set so as to maximize the flow of goods through narrow and heavily used sea-lanes. Such a scheme would be based on commonality of interest in safe navigation rather than on the allocation of jurisdictional rights between coastal and flag states.

Efforts to delineate a desirable regime for *deep-sea mining* are complicated by the fact that the issue has become highly politicized as well as by the fact that unrealistic expectations have been generated concerning the financial returns from deep-sea mining. These expectations center upon the creation of a rather sizable international seabed mining authority composed of various technical commissions, an assembly, a council, a secretariat, a tribunal, and an enterprise that will operate, in effect, as a mining company. Substantial differences regarding the role of state or private mining companies vis-à-vis the authority in general and the enterprise in particular separate the industrialized from the developing states. The regimes proposed by both sides in the debate are based on exaggerated estimates of the prospects for deep-sea mining and are faulty in terms of one or more criteria for a desirable mining system.

To arrive at a regime that would optimize the benefits to be derived from ocean mining, it is necessary to build on the facts that are presently available regarding the costs of mining and the likely world-market prices for nickel, cobalt, copper, and manganese. Present evidence suggests that even in a favorable legal environment, technical difficulties in initiating a new operation combined with the relatively low price of land-based minerals will result in the slow growth of nodule mining. Some estimates suggest approximately 10 to 15 million tons of ore would be mined by the mid-1980s and around 50 million tons by the year 2000. Because availability of the technology remains uncertain and capital costs high, deep-sea mining on this scale, although feasible, may not be highly profitable.[9] Thus legal measures that

[9]Calculations of profitability vary significantly among analysts who have made projections of returns on deep-sea mining. Richard Cooper estimates that by 1985, 10 million dry metric tons of ore will be recovered annually. In constant

increase the uncertainties plus substantial taxes on mining will simply discourage development of the resource. While this might provide higher returns for the few land-based producers, it will not optimize overall material well-being. To achieve this goal requires a regime that would allow deep-sea mining to develop as its cost approached that of land-based mining. The multinational companies that own the technology should be neither hindered nor subsidized in their undertaking. The minerals should become available to the international community through existing world markets.

Such an approach, although it may be efficient in the production of resources for the market, does not resolve the inequities inherent in a situation where a few industrialized countries possess the technology and therefore the revenues (as distinct from the product) from mining. The question of perceptions of equity and of national dignity may be addressed through the allocation of revenues and participation in the international decision-making machinery that will regulate mineral exploitation and revenue disbursement. To generate international revenues without deterring mining, a tax should be levied on gross revenues along

---

1976 dollars and using 1976 costs and prices, he estimates a net revenue for a three-metal operation (copper, cobalt, nickel) of $20 per dry metric ton or a total annual net revenue of $200 million in 1985. Richard N. Cooper, "The Oceans as a Source of Revenue," in Jagdish Bhagwati (ed.), *The New International Economic Order: The North-South Debate*, MIT Press, Cambridge, Mass., 1977.

Danny Leipziger and James Mudge have estimated that 15 million dry metric tons will be recovered annually by 1985. One million of this will be a seven-metal operation (copper, cobalt, nickel, manganese, vanadium, zinc, molybdenum) and 14 million will be a three-metal operation. Using constant 1974 dollars and estimated 1985 costs and prices, they calculate a net revenue for a seven-metal operation of between $185 and $253 per dry metric ton and for a three-metal operation of between $58 and $109 per dry metric ton. Annual net revenues in 1985 based on this calculation would range from $997 to $1,779 million. Danny M. Leipziger and James L. Mudge, *Seabed Mineral Resources and the Economic Interests of Developing Countries*, Ballinger, Cambridge, Mass., 1976.

the lines of normal corporate profits taxes, that is, at a rate of 50 percent.[10] The tax would represent an international tax on what would essentially be international corporations. As in the case of other overseas operations, the tax should be credited against domestic tax liabilities. The revenues that would be generated by an international corporate tax could range between $100 and $900 million per year by the mid-1980s. These revenues might be put to any of a number of uses. Initially they should be used to cover the costs of the international machinery needed to regulate deep-sea mining on behalf of the international community. In addition, it might be deemed politically desirable to create an international enterprise to mine the seabed. The revenues could then be directed to securing the necessary technology, equipment, and personnel to make the enterprise operational. If the decision is made to create an international operating body, it would be purely on the ground that such an enterprise would allow those countries to participate directly in deep-sea mining that otherwise would be unable to do so. This participation might contribute to their perceptions of national dignity, but it should not be allowed to reduce the material benefits that can be expected to accrue to all from deep-sea mining. As revenues grow beyond the year 2000, there might be additional revenues available to produce international public goods.

The use to which ocean-mining revenues are put should be determined by the member nations of the international community on the premise that the resources of the seabed are the common heritage of mankind. Unfortunately, the projected revenues from nodule mining will not go far to cover the ambitious schemes for simultaneously developing an enterprise *and* an elaborate international authority in the near future. Increasingly aware of these financial limitations, members of the Group of 77 have sought to extract promises of financing and mandatory transfer of technology from the affluent and the industrialized countries. This strategy holds little promise of success, given the

[10]An alternative way of generating revenues would be via an auction system, including an initial fee and a tax on outputs. This approach, however, might be better applied when the number of potential competitors for seabed mining has grown.

readiness of a number of developed nations to scrap the negotiations and to begin mining on their own. Thus, if there is to be an enterprise as well as an international authority, the financing will probably have to come from the revenues generated by mining. (The submission of two prospective mine sites by companies seeking a license from the authority constitutes a form of revenue to finance the enterprise.) This suggests that a streamlined international authority would be the first institution to be established and that the enterprise would begin to function only after the 1980s, when sufficient revenues made it possible to acquire the needed personnel and technology. Whenever it did come into being, the enterprise as well as the international authority would provide an opportunity for the participation of all nations in decision making regarding seabed mining. However the decision-making machinery were structured, it should provide for the representation of the various resource-related interests of nations, and it should be subject to periodic revision to allow for new and different interests to be represented if and when they developed.

This preferred regime for the management of the oceans—fisheries, hydrocarbons, environment, shipping, and deep-sea minerals—attempts to maximize overall material well-being through management policies appropriate to the physical characteristics and technological facts of each resource. By distinguishing between four distinct aspects of resource use, it should be possible to disentangle the complex problems raised by national preoccupations with status and dignity. The use of a resource involves the process of exploitation, the disposition of the product, the generation and disposition of revenues, and the process of decision making concerning some or all of these activities. Participation in the decision-making process as well as sharing in the revenues generated by resource use may satisfy national concerns over dignity in some resource-management schemes. In others, only direct participation in the process of exploitation may serve this end. An oceans regime that maximizes overall material well-being and satisfies the less tangible national concerns with dignity is likely to provide the additional benefit of certainty or predictability in the continued enjoyment of ocean resources.

THE PATH FROM THE PRESENT TO A PREFERRED
FUTURE REGIME

The precise details of an oceans regime for mining, fishing, and the like must be developed cooperatively. Because views differ as to what is an ideal regime and because international cooperation will be avoided where states think they can better advance their interests unilaterally, there is no assurance that anything approximating an ideal oceans regime can be achieved. Nonetheless, it is possible to envision the major steps that must be taken to get from the present and prospective oceans regime to one that is better in terms of global material well-being, national dignity, and certainty.

Three principal objectives must be pursued: (1) A division of almost 50 percent of ocean space into exclusively national zones must not be sanctioned in an international treaty. (2) The work of international technical oceans organizations must be resumed, revised, and strengthened. (3) The United States either independently or in conjunction with neighboring states and other developed states must begin to implement the principles of wise management in its own policies.

UNCLOS is entering its seventh year, and a reversal of trends therein would be difficult, to be sure. Nonetheless, a growing number of geographically disadvantaged countries have gradually come to realize that what has been dubbed by one commentator as "the great riparian rip-off" will be grossly inequitable. If the United States were to reverse its present policy of extending its jurisdiction as far into the oceans as possible, it might generate the necessary support among these states to avoid international approbation of the present spatial-jurisdictional approach to an oceans regime.

To avert finalizing a division of the oceans will not be enough. A positive program must be initiated as well. That will require an effort on the international, regional, and national fronts simultaneously. At the international level the work of an ongoing overall Law of the Sea forum should be harmonized with that of strengthened technical bodies. The Law of the Sea Conference and its preparatory committee have served to educate a number

202

of small nations as to oceans problems and their interests therein. It should continue to meet annually to review developments of the preceding months and to consider and approve international agreements prepared within appropriate technical bodies. These bodies, the Food and Agriculture Organization, the Intergovernmental Maritime Consultative Organization, the Intergovernmental Oceanographic Commission (IOC), an international seabed authority, and the International Energy Agency (IEA), should proceed to consider the development of appropriate management regimes in their respective areas of competence. Historically, most of these bodies have been given little authority to determine and enforce management regulations. The United States has been foremost among those reluctant to cede an ounce of authority to international regulatory bodies it does not control. If an ideal oceans regime is to be achieved, this historical practice will have to be reversed, and the United States will have to lead the way. This it could do immediately in the regional bodies that will have to be established to properly manage fisheries and environmental problems. The semi-enclosed waters of the Caribbean are at the top of the list of those areas where United States regional cooperation is imperative.

The United States must also lead the way in those areas where a multilateral approach is not dictated by physical interdependencies. When commercial recovery of petroleum beyond 200-meter depths begins off its own shores, the United States should set aside a substantial portion of revenues to help finance the IEA, an international seabed authority, or international development banks. In so doing, the United States government should seek the collaboration of other developed nations of the Northern Hemisphere. By setting an example of how to implement the concept of common heritage, wider participation in such an approach may develop over time. The same holds true for revenues gained from regional management of fisheries.

While the United States cannot determine the policies that will be pursued by other states, it can, so to speak, put its own house in order. By implementing wise management policies in its own use of ocean resources, and by encouraging international cooperation in this approach, the United States may set an example that would be difficult for other countries to ignore.

Selected Bibliography

Connelly, P., and R. Perlman: *The Politics of Scarcity*, Royal Institute of International Affairs, Oxford University Press, London, 1975.

Cooper, Richard N.: "The Oceans as a Source of Revenues," in Jagdish Bhagwati (ed.), *The New International Economic Order: The North-South Debate*, MIT Press, Cambridge, Mass., 1977.

Díaz-Alejandro, Carlos F.: "North-South Relations: The Economic Component,"*International Organization,* vol. 29, Winter 1975, pp. 213–241.

Fried, Edward R.: "International Trade in Raw Materials: Myths and Realities," *Science*, vol. 191, February 20, 1976, pp. 641–646.

International Economic Studies Institute: *Raw Materials and Foreign Policy*, IESI, Washington, D.C., 1976.

Johnson, Harry G.: *Economic Policies Toward Less Developed Countries*, The Brookings Institution, Washington, D.C., 1967.

Law, Alton D.: *International Commodity Agreements*, Lexington Books, Lexington, Mass., 1975.

Leipziger, Danny M., and James L. Mudge: *Seabed Mineral Resources and Economic Interests of Developing Countries*, Ballinger Publishing Co., Cambridge, Mass, 1976.

MacBean, Alasdair I.: *Export Instability and Economic Development*, Harvard University Press, Cambridge, Mass., 1966.

Mikdashi, Zuhayr: *The International Politics of Natural Resources*, Cornell University Press, Ithaca, N.Y., 1976.

Mikesell, Raymond F.: "More Third World Cartels Ahead?" *Challenge*, vol. 17, November/December 1974, pp. 24–31.

Morton, Kathryn, and Peter Tulloch: *Trade and Developing Countries*, Croom Helm, London, 1977.

Novick, David, et al.: *A World of Scarcities*, Associated Business Programmes, London, 1976.

Osgood, Robert E., et al.: *Toward a National Ocean Policy: 1976 and Beyond*, Report of the Johns Hopkins Ocean Policy Project to the National Science Foundation, U.S. Government Printing Office, Washington, D.C., 1976.

Pardo, Arvid: "A Statement on the Future Law of the Sea in Light of Current Trends and Negotiations," *Ocean Development and International Law*, vol. 1, no. 4, Winter 1974, pp. 315–335.

Ruggie, John Gerard, and Ernst B. Haas (eds.): "International Responses to Technology," *International Organization*, vol. 29, no. 3, Summer 1975, pp. 557–583.

Trilateral Commission: *A New Regime for the Oceans*, A Report of the Trilateral Task Force on the Oceans, December 1975.

Index

About the Authors

RUTH W. ARAD is a lecturer at the Graduate School of Business Administration of Tel Aviv University. She received her Ph.D. in statistics from Princeton University in 1975. Before moving to Israel, she worked as an operations research analyst with Morgan Guaranty Trust in New York.

UZI B. ARAD is currently a lecturer in the political science department and an associate with the Center for Strategic Studies at Tel Aviv University. Dr. Arad received his Ph.D. in politics from Princeton University in 1975. Before moving to Israel, he worked as a professional staff member of the Hudson Institute in New York.

RACHEL McCULLOCH is associate professor of economics at Harvard University. Professor McCulloch received her Ph.D. in economics from the University of Chicago in 1973. Her publications include articles on tariff preferences, technology transfer, primary commodity trade, and other aspects of North-South economic relations.

JOSÉ PIÑERA has been a professor of economics at the Catholic University of Chile since 1975 and a visiting professor at the Center for Latin American Development Studies at Boston University since 1974. He is also editor of *Economia y Sociedad* and has served as a UN Development Programme regional advisor on export promotion policies. Dr. Piñera is the author of several articles on trade and export policies. He received his M.A. and Ph.D. in economics from Harvard University.

ANN L. HOLLICK is currently at the Congressional Research Service of the Library of Congress as a specialist in ocean policy. Prior to this position she was an associate professor of international law and organization; the executive director of the Ocean Policy Project at Johns Hopkins University; and, in 1977, the Treasury member of the U.S. Delegation to the UN Conference on the Law of the Sea. She is the author of numerous articles on ocean policy and has written *Toward a National Ocean Policy: 1976 and Beyond* (co-author) and *Marine Policy, Law and Economics: Annotated Bibliography.*

EDWARD L. MORSE is Special Assistant to the Under Secretary for Economic Affairs, Department of State. He was formerly Executive Director of the 1980s Project of the Council on Foreign Relations.